CW00348611

NEW POETRIES VIII

In 1969 Michael Schmidt was a founder of Carcanet Press, where he remains Editorial Director and has been associated with all eight *New Poetries* anthologies. He is also an editor of the magazine *PN Review*, a poet, literary historian and teacher.

John McAuliffe is an Irish poet whose collections include, most recently, *The Kabul Olympics* (Gallery Press) and his versions of the Bosnian poet Igor Klikovac, *Stockholm Syndrome* (Smith|Doorstop). He is also an editor of the magazine *PN Review*, Associate Publisher at Carcanet and Professor of Poetry at the University of Manchester's Centre for New Writing.

III

N E W   P O E T R I E S

AN ANTHOLOGY

edited by

MICHAEL SCHMIDT
& JOHN MCAULIFFE

CARCANET

First published in Great Britain in 2021
by Carcanet, 30 Cross Street
Manchester M2 7AQ
www.carcanet.co.uk

A CIP catalogue record for this book is
available from the British Library.

ISBN 978 1 80017 040 7

Book design by Andrew Latimer
Printed in Great Britain by SRP Ltd, Exeter, Devon

The publisher acknowledges financial
assistance from Arts Council England.

CONTENTS

An Intrepid Cloud in June

If you read poetry every day, and then add in the hundreds of poets, thousands of poems under consideration for an anthology, you quickly start to privilege and value certain effects: those images which almost stammeringly refuse to take their leave; insistent rhythms sustained line after line; the knitting together of form and tone where tone presides; poems so engaging you want them to keep going and never stop. It becomes fascinating to see how one stand-out poem is accompanied, how a poet who writes one complete poem writes others, too.

Our conversations, our enthusiasms, singled out the poems and poets we chose. We did certainly go looking for new voices, believing that poets generally operate at an angle to communities. And reading back over this anthology, its abundance surprises, as does its good unruliness.

In 'Education of the Poet' Louise Glück, who has championed so many poets at the start of their careers, writes about growing up in 'the worst possible family', an 'environment in which the right of any family member to complete the sentence of another was assumed […] in my family all discussion was carried on in that single cooperative voice.' *New Poetries VIII* is not this kind of family and, even as we attempt to identify common elements, these poets as a group happily insist on completing their own sentences.

And so it should be. Carcanet grew out of the eponymous student magazine Michael took over in 1967 as an undergraduate. As Michael has recently written: 'The Press was intended to be a brief, decisive swansong: to publish pamphlets by a few poets whose work Carcanet had encouraged, and then stop. But at the time poetry publishing was hardly

thriving. New presses emerged – Fulcrum and Anvil in par-
ticular – but old lists were cautious, some were closing. Poets
were in peril of losing, or had lost, publishers. There were po-
ets from abroad, Anglophone and other, who ought to have
been part of our diet. When *Poetry Nation*, then *PN Review*
got going, the press was caught up in a hopeless enthusiasm
which persists.

Carcanet has been backward- and forward-looking at the
same time. Age and experience do not count against poets; and
we had, and have, a weak spot for poet-critics. Being British or
belonging to a specific school did not matter. We were at odds
with the then "establishment". The editorial principle then as
now is, Wait to be surprised. Submissions which make you
read aloud are off to a good start. If they surprise by rightness,
and by a relation to larger traditions, modernist or otherwise,
they engage us.

Particularism would be our philosophy, if we had one.
It entails a resistance to theories and "schools", to family
resemblances. To say more would risk a limiting definition…'

In this eighth anthology, the poets share a canny sense of the
neighbourhood in which they exercise their gift, not unaware
of language's systems and tendencies, and history's surprises
(Brexit, say, or a pandemic), which might suddenly illuminate
or shadow or anyway redefine the ways in which the poems
will be read. Jade Cuttle might speak for many of them,
and us, when she draws our attention to her poems' interest
in 'the unruly self', and their resistance to 'flatpacking the
endless contradictions of identity into one single neat space'.
Stav Poleg prefaces her poems' cinematic scene-switching
with Wittgenstein's own meditation on the self's protean
shapeshifting: 'When one means something, it is oneself
that means,' before declaring, 'The process of working on a
poem often feels to me like that of getting lost.' This book's

twenty-four poets might be considered as invitations, for the time you spend in their company, to lose yourself.

The failures of the Baedeker or Lonely Planet have long been a prompt to poets: Tristram Fane Saunders writes, 'The guidebook says so many things, but we can't hear it / over the water falling everywhere and on the blue pagoda.' He insists on the undiscovered, the overlooked spaces, hidden tones and feelings to which his poems attest. It might be Christine Roseeta Walker's Negril, Jamaica or the Catalan and Wexford silences in which Colm Tóibín's poems specialise, or the Suffolk landscape, or better, *world* of Rebecca Hurst's 'Mapping the Woods':

> Count the ways in:
> the tracks and driftways,
> sheere-ways and bostals,
> gaps, twittens and stiles.
> Loop round and back again.
> These Wealden hills burn us up
> – the effort of taking them in the snow

Maybe we can see in these poems a poetics that stresses other worlds, and how the poems' speakers acknowledge habitats and lives, and language, other than their own. Jade Cuttle's alphabet tilts at the very basis of what written language does, its foraging and re-orientation matched by Nell Prince's 'Isle', which asks us to notice otherworldly poplars that will become 'our judges / before the bone silence, the no-return'. For Jenny King in 'Point of Balance', our focus, at best, is 'a balancing, attention / pulled thinly sideways as the moments pass.' The brilliant, iconic poems of Jason Allen-Paisant also pull sideways, asking us, demanding of us: 'Imagine daffodils in the corner / of a sound system / in Clapham'.

These poets do not just imagine other ways of seeing, they also bring all their wit and formal resources to bear on difficult inheritances and other histories. How hard it is to get things down right! Parwana Fayyaz achieves this with her remarkable litanies, which haunt her poems' occasions, as do both the Iranian and Mancunian scenes of Maryam Hessavi's, and Joseph Minden's playful sonnet sequences and painful meditations on what is forgotten, and what is memorialised.

As we read these selected poems and poets together one unusual preoccupation dominated, perhaps related to the larger sense that we are writers of the Anthropocene: the draw of tides and elemental water for these poets' imagining of another world. Benjamin Nehammer's coastal cityscapes notice 'quiet reaches of the surf / Stranger and stranger in the reeds'; Charlotte Eichler entangles the human and animal worlds, her cuttlefish

> speak a patterned language
> of moody stripes and flashes,
> the signs of love imprinted
> on their skin,

> leave their eggs
> like a dropped necklace,
> ruffled versions of themselves
> suspended in each blackened bead.

Joe Carrick-Varty wishfully interweaves private disaster and non-human vitality: 'Every time a whale is born albino / a man doesn't die of liver failure and every time / it rains at sea a child speaks first words'; Jennifer Edgecombe's voice-driven poems inhabit that seascape: 'I asked him when he'll be round the corner / we call Land's End the corner / he said about just after tea'; Holly Hopkins' North American Loon 'will shoot her call like a flare / and it will hang / over the office workers of Whitehall'; Suzannah V. Evans's amazing starfish and barnacles have the gift of being utterly at home in their environment:

> Barnacles balancing though tightly balancing
> breathing and balancing and barnacled
> brittle blushes all spiny and together and a beginning
> beginning to merge the brittle blushing objects, all briny.

These poems might wish for such easy belonging, but they register instead a separateness which can be confrontational, or neighbourly, or, sometimes, passionately identifying and engaged.

One of Padraig Regan's ingenious, passionate poems about what we eat, 'Katsu Ika Odori-Don', observes the preparation of a squid dish: horrified, drawn in, it is also a meditation on elegiac distance: 'I know what animates this bunch of tentacles: / it's just the salt in the soy filling the blanks in the dead nerves.' Isobel Williams's startlingly inventive Catullus relishes both the body and its own attempts to resuscitate, decorate and despoil its subjects: 'I'll squirt correctly spelt obscene graffiti / All over your façade', she writes; Conor Cleary's recycling is more practical, a stove emerging from cans as he 'punctured neat holes in them with a corkscrew / and poured in a bright purple ethanol', while Victoria Kennefick's dramatic monologues bring such transformations of speech and body very close together: her St Catherine exclaims,

> Oh, Bonaventura, I am a house of sticks,
> my bones rattle with desire until I lick it.
> I feel it quiver, alive on my tongue.

Swapping poems and notes in a locked down northern city, this profligate Babel of new poetries emerged out of the tidal swells it still withstands: we came back again and again to the pleasures the poets afforded us, to the suddenness with which their poems spoke to us, something caught by Hal Coase's 'The Beginnings':

> I like poems that start with a bird stuck in a chimneybreast
>   or even better in a living room
> where everyone's screaming and there's purple shit
>   everywhere and mum acknowledges the problem,
>   ideally
>   with an old-school touch of humour:
>   'And who invited you?'

John McAuliffe
2021

NEW POETRIES VIII

It's said that in the first offices of Amazon's PN13 team, the department responsible for 'personalisation' (that is, the algorithmic use of your data to generate higher sales), there was a sign that read: 'People forget that John Henry died in the end'. Of course, we don't. Zora Neale Hurston's version in *Polk County* has the steel-driving man's death and its mourning as the ballad's reason for being sung.

John Henry's story – real or mythic; real, then mythic – and the arrival of the 'big machines' in his place, would not have gotten very far without his death. Without it, perhaps, the machines really would have won. I love the camp menace of that Amazon sign (real or mythic), the easy intensity with which it announces the irrelevance of storytelling and the irony of a reminder that people forget. It has worked for me as a challenge and a model – to address real dangers with that same tone.

If the poems here register a recurrent concern, it will be an interest in what loss, guilt and depersonalisation have to do with each other. Poems that I read again and again often bring together, in tense contrast, the senses of estrangement and attachment which can suddenly form in moments of loss. They don't resolve and they don't settle. There is only what O'Hara had down as 'the dead hunting / and the alive, ahunted' – the slip of 'haunted' into a more menacing, vital rush of action.

The story of John Henry at Amazon HQ tells me something about the dangers of forgetting or, worse, remembering badly. 'We are all in danger', as Pasolini had it – in danger of being misunderstood and misnamed, with language as misleader-in-chief.

*

THE BEGINNINGS

I like poems that start with a bird stuck in a chimneybreast
      or even better in a living room
where everyone's screaming and there's purple shit
        everywhere and mum acknowledges the problem,
        ideally
        with an old-school touch of humour:
            'And who invited you?'

and I like paintings that start with Anne Bancroft's eyes
      on John the Baptist – said eyes should be
aware of this miracle – or failing that
appalled by the mix-up and desperate
           to get out of the wilderness
and back to a cigarette in Central Park
      and where there's blood
      it should have something to do with revenge
for elocution lessons.

Dance I don't know anything about but in my opinion the best ones start
by taking someone's hand
      and then realise this hand is not their sister's hand
but go on holding it anyway because embarrassment
is for adults and if they're lucky
they'll make a new friend
and then their sister will buy them something irreplaceable
      so that they don't tell the adults.

The songs I like, I like because they start by locking themselves out of
      their flat by accident
and so after trying to climb the fire-escape,
then arguing with the neighbour who has always hated their relaxed
approach to parenting appointments
and basic peacetime security measures,

have to spend hours and hours
        walking the block, kicking imaginary cans,
before remembering an old two-timing lover
        who has a spare key and going round theirs just as it gets dark.

I like plays that start three minutes late, right after
        we find the seats, our cheeks still flushing.

Movies, I like the ones that start with a body
in a swimming pool, the fedora still on,
        that's good – or better yet a montage of bodies in swimming pools
from different eras (some with extremely elaborate Persian tiling),
or else I like the ones that simply start
with someone walking through an airport, someone who looks like they
   could say
        'I love you' for ninety minutes straight
        and you wouldn't get too bored,
        more incredibly they wouldn't either,
or when not possible then I like the ones that start the way Lina Wertmüller
makes them start since she can start a movie smoother than
        the world can turn. I can't stand movies that start
        with someone sitting down to write a novel, and vice versa,
though more vice than versa.

I like novels that start with an insincere apology for being late –
        they were 'leaving to come and join you
            but then remembered the market was on
            and took a detour' kind of thing and you didn't even know
there was a market in this town but now
here they are with exceptional dates as proof,
and also hoarse and smug from an afternoon of haggling for the hell of it,
something that doesn't appeal one bit
        but you'd be happy to have seen.
Books – books most generally speaking should start with déjà vu.

And days well I like days that start anywhichway
but if I had to chose
I'd start with appearances –
        so no rain, locusts, cloches, frogs, etc. does this look good to you?
this also rules out meek days,
days that have been bullied by their season –
we want an intrepid cloud in June and a November rainbow that starts out of
    sight
and in keeping with the dream
        I just finished is shaggy and downmarket and has a stroke of burgundy
        and ends goodness knows where

RECORD, RECORD

The photographer resists the undertow.
His hands speak for him. They keep time
with his thought.

I can stand beside him there in the lowering
sun, as the trees begin to lean on tomorrow,
unnoticed by them.

I am quiet, I've counted chattel in the past,
then cleaned up neighbourhoods and not once
been seen at all.

There's a little talk of fore- and backgrounds,
not worth the writing down, before the shot is taken
and whiteness frames

everything with an equal lack, the world bled dry
of colour. We all cheer. It is fun and games
and night again.

We can well imagine how the loaded image
stales too soon and goes bad in the memory.
What do you get?

An honest souvenir: a gentle, documented look.
You pass the time in it gladly, as if sleeping a decade
after the massacres end.

ESCAPED

She carried you all
the way from home, Sundays too,
             with a high fever.

In your hot ears she
sang neutrally of strong men
             who will not look back.

Outside metaphors
burned – a whole town on its knees
             to ask for prayers.

Her song was in this
but also out of danger;
             a fire seen from space,

a black collecting
what its owed, raising questions
                    after dried answers.

She has left us here
some beginnings to choose from
                    or to leave behind.

ON DISSEMINATION

admittedly, this was a man who knew the names of fifteen
     different axes – felling,
hatchet, hafted, splitting, tomahawk, crash, hewing, adze,
     flensing, mattock, pick,
bearded, broad, labrys – I cut him off, 'What's your favourite
     seed?' Then, him:
nothing would be grown anymore, the cutting times had
     never even paused,
this was the downward swing, the weight would do the work,
     your hands
were academic, and, would I excuse him, he had other
     customers waiting. I planted
nothing that year because I couldn't find the exit; the logs
     stacked up like debt.

SEBASTIAN

in anticipation he turned on all the lamps
& out went all the overhead lighting
this made his body both covert & lambent

like the balloons used to convey dispatches
over the heads of royalists besieging
paris in 1871 which were both covert

& lambent since the firelight of the camps
surrounding the city struck their white
ribbons as they passed by he was exactly

like that but with a glass of wine & extremely
limited knowledge of the siege of paris
in 1871 which was fine by him how odd he

thought nakedness is so odd

LAYTIME

Not wishing to exaggerate, the car alarm
stops eventually. That neglectful calm
is back. It is my favourite time of day,
when our walk says nothing so exactly,
the new strains to anchor, cargo's sent
upstream and neither are then dreamt on.
For the love of this, let our looks
        in sleep be but always raised
        and gutted like a statue's gaze.

2ND JANUARY

Reading by the candle of life
we complete his ledgers

John Berger

It was just evening
on a coastal path
in the country where
you found a home
to live through.
The view was what
you'd notice in it:
vines, roots, dirt,
stories, touchable
and tended to.

I could have met
you at the turn
talking of love
with a labourer.
I would have known
you, secretary, by
that 'I don't know
but I imagine so.'
Your doubts held
hope like January.

You might have
stopped to voice
the soil's unheard
work, draw its
fruits beneath
a borderless blue
and listen as if life

depended on it
(far oftener than not,
it does, you knew).

THE GUILTY PARTY

The powers that were announce the end of power.

It was an afternoon of criminal celebration

with levels of sweat, proficient theft and dance not seen since the
descent of power.

People of the town debunked into sand-track streets
from their cabanas

to make together love, eye-contact, and excuses.

We were told: it is like the sixties – without teeth
or clothes.

The mayor revealed he was losing his mind: 'I am
losing my mind!' he explained over intercom,

so everyone hurried to provide him with sympathy blankets and
confiscate his golf clubs.

They established a university, which was a place with
clean drinking water,

and it was named after power. It was the best time to be alive;

even the dead signed a petition with words to that effect.

ARRIVED

We did not know
it would leave us
here. Our sun sits
bored as a dog
at noon, gnawing
the dirt.

No stir, no. From
here, the earth may
as well be flat –
this eye its centre,
this needled head
its lode,

all horizons
drop down and off.
I'm not yet a
parvenu; I
am still searching
the heat

which stops here not
much further than
the reach of my
arm – dislocated,
artless wing
beating

off this young light,
caught by the sun,
that attrition
of seen things, which
comes home safe
and sound.

ADRIA

Our words are the children of many people.

Giorgos Seferis

I will never see your ocean,
those queryings you laid on it
might by now have floated out
to a port of grey mangrove
with a clear-eyed fisherman
hidden in its thicket's stretch.

That is: a dream from a city,
where your sounds break in
like a wave shoaled up to begin

RECCO

after Eugenio Montale

Spring: the reed lets go
    its longest red leaves.
    The path of a dry creek
    fills with dragonflies;
    the dog schleps home,
    a winning in his gob.

Today I couldn't recognise this place,
but there where the heat rises
and the clouds tilt, your eyes,
by now distant, seem only
two points of light
                and time comes on.

CANNAREGIO

from a Hebrew prayer

If nothing is ahead
but our ready lips,

recall how pain
sounds a way out,

the bravery of it:
its blind beginning.

How he said
to the child:

'Take fire to the altar,
place incense and run
to the people. Forgive.'

How he stood
between those gone

and the living
until it ended
and he returned.

CHAGALL'S FABLES IN EUROPE

I am about to feel if only the past were simpler – after all, it's as finished as a
hand held up in surrender, but then there is its body
dragged from the wrist, down to a shoulder lent on the border that admits
no light every etch is giving me a new no way out
but happily this lamb is out leading the slaughter. In another summer,
narration drowns itself in an untellable tub – here's the proof,
in our summer, a hot & fresh heaven, that every eye's a wager for humanity
& knowing sleep like we do is trust in the world-
as-will-be. I feel about the instincts of the fox, grope for a sympathetic fang
to pull me up – because there's good news outside, for once
we're able to mend our cynicism & make it new but inside the animals are
straight-faced, they want food not hope, the funny side
is one big wound, it turns your stomach. You've got some pity stuck between
your teeth.

FOR A HETEROPESSIMIST

I'm not qualified for this kind of
honesty, that's the truth. Demonstrate
with a thrust of humour like a frog on
a highway. But as a child, we all felt it –
no? How I wish to try harder to come
in a room like a man looking to buy a
room but what if mum saw and joking
aside we had to share the self-image
forever? 'It's something to write home
about,' adds the dealer in what has
been established as his third language.
This was a thing to say to a me running
from every crumb of home, but since his
accent took naivety to task and since he
wasn't to know about the family putsch
at the funeral and since, moreover, I felt
suddenly at ease amidst the flat's bare
hostility, I began admiring the skirting
boards. 'You are admiring the skirting
boards,' he says. I blush, embarrassed at
having been seen admiring the skirting
boards. They are scuffed, not admirable,
the scuffs are gorgeous browns; the edge
is hardy.

NOTES FROM A POOL BOY

What is it about a pool in the Bay Area?
First, that I've never seen one and neither, as far as I know,
have you or Dimitris Yeros. Maybe it's existence
'as a matter   *Hannah Black*
of degree' – just so: a dive into that cool from that heat
even with my clothes on plus 8000 miles to make up,
is too happy to leave untouched. Or else it's the 'Where had I
passed the night?' of getting up, hard   *Tommaso Giartosio*
and surrounded by smoke
which rises on the highway out of shot
and tired of most years
becoming good graves
to be attended when we need them,
and a dive, a real dive –

or I would be the swimmer on their way from home –
all the ways to the other coast, cracking the surface,
manic as my father's last eyes, until I am a weed
at your feet, netted and hung to dry by chance
in the too much sun. The whole neighbourhood,
in Atlantean style, flopping commentary, stood over mocktails,
asking: 'Was he beautiful or not
beautiful? and what was the secret of form
or expression
which gave the dynamic quality to his stroke?'   *George Eliot*

there is a danger that even you wouldn't recognise me,
so careered and concluded. And that is part of it – a risk
in the offing – *With His Thoughts On* escape
into others. But simply look at it: we can't do the day
without the make-believe, the dry land of burnt crops of future histories

under us and the skies in various states of undress
and water ready to be broken, distressed,
if I'm allowed
the violence of that image.

*

HAL COASE is a playwright and poet. He completed an MA
in Creative Writing at the University of Manchester in 2018.
His pamphlet *Laytime* was shortlisted for the *White Review*
Poet's Prize in the same year. In 2019 he received a grant from
Arts Council England to support the development of a first
collection. His plays, published by Oberon Books, have been
performed at the Camden People's Theatre, the Pleasance
Theatre and the Arcola. He lives in Bologna, Italy.

'The poem is always a record of failure.' This sad logic is derived via Allen Grossman's story about 'the song of the infinite' being 'compromised by the finitude of its terms'. There's conflict between the poet's desire to make an alternative world and 'resistance [...] inherent in the materials of which any world must be composed'. At the most basic level, these materials are the ink and paper that constitute the two-dimensional presentation of language. No matter how imaginative or original the usage, words can never extend beyond the bracken-fringed thicket of thought to overcome the flatness of the page, and represent with genuine authenticity the multi-dimensional complexity of existence.

This 'record of failure' lamented by Ben Lerner comes into focus, in the case of these poems, when crafting a representation of the self and the lyric 'I' (identity; a performative illusion that adapts according to environment and entourage). In Claudia Rankine's *Citizen*, Rankine writes about the lyric 'I' falling short of its intention; striving to flatpack the endless contradictions of identity into one single neat space, yet ultimately failing to 'hold the person together'. As Denise Riley writes, each time a poet chooses to package their identity into the narrow confines of the lyric 'I', they are 'subjecting [themselves] to subjectification'; choosing to portray one of their potential identities over another.

In terms of gender identity, Hélène Cixous argues that 'woman' has always occupied a position of otherness and alterity in Western phallogocentric culture. I would argue that this position becomes further removed into alterity when selfhood is plagued by a similar phenomenon, linked, for example, to complex relations with notions of race or class.

In French, '*être en décalage*', as referenced in these poems, means to be out of phase with something, though here I advance the notion of being out of phase (or othered) from oneself. Mixed-race, multicultural and multi-lingual, constantly moving between countries, cultures and languages in search of 'home', I relate to this coining more than any English equivalent; the '*dé*' emphasising the sense of dislodgement these poems seek to convey.

The compulsively neat, box-like poetic form aims to create an aesthetically satisfying organisation (categorisation; exercise of power) that is robotically at odds with the organic nature of human bodies, their 'home' and, specifically, these chaotic self-portraits; in order to emphasise the dissonance in selfhood that drives their creation.

My creative impulse snags on the edges of each 'I'; that unshakeable anchor, scudding along its sentence, until the contradictions of lyric integrity are exposed. As I set about casting the lyric 'I' away from the crowd of words that keep it warm; blindly bowing down beneath its totemic authority, to interrogate the real standing of the lyric 'I' left stranded and shivering without a script, I become more interested in exploring self-expression as a medium; interrogating its limits and its lies.

In the extract from the alphabet sequence, the metaphorical organisation of each poem is based around the history of one letter from the alphabet. This metaphor is then transmuted into a situation that corresponds to the story I want to tell. The aim is to examine the impact of colonial language, how it is tamed to suit people's purposes but does not suit people's purposes equally. As Riley writes, 'There's a terrific and cheerfully direct statement of this intimacy between shame and song.'

In a similar vein to the French poet Henri Michaux's expedition into his internal 'espace du dedans': 'travelling in myself – that is the adventure of being alive', I work to unlock hidden dimensions of identity; unravelling the unruly self, most often, through the lens of ecopoetic language.

The Korean poet Kim Kyung Ju has offered an illuminating entry into how such ideas can be explored through ecopoetry. This poet's manifold layering of landscapes – corporeal onto countryside, compiled as though composed of tracing paper – creates 'a shared sense of the death / of our singular selves', a concept at which my poems converge.

In mapping external and internal landscapes together, I pursue an extended sense of self that buffers and scrapes against surroundings. I work to redraft the notion of the eco-tone, where habitats merge (Clifford; King), until topography extends to include mixed-race emotion and experience, and place becomes porous and relational (Massey; Lippard) to psychological realms. The sprawling sinister subplot in these poems works to redraft expectations surrounding the aesthetically sublime, challenging the notion that nature must always be a tranquil place of retreat, when used to map complex self-portraits distorted by restrictive notions of race, gender and class.

I would even argue that ecopoetry's ability to illuminate hidden aspects of identity is actually coded beyond content into the fundamental stratigraphical properties of poetic form. Beneath the surface decoration of ecopoetic language, lies a formal framework whose diverse layers invite a foraging approach to the extraction of meaning. I see the process of entering such ecopoems; foraging through its layers for meaning, for answers, then re-emerging with a renewed sense of awareness, as deeply nourishing and vital.

*

THISTLE & BONE

I am thistle and bone – occupied
by weeds, those anxious warriors no
one wants to grow; unyielding, they
wield a sharp-edged tongue even
I am pained to swallow. Sieged
by feuding shoots, we wrestle, one
stalk yanked by sun, the other by
shade - a limb-tearing punishment
worthy of medieval applause. Even
those spindly rosy-cheekers are
scheming between themselves; I
can hear the clasp of flesh, roots
tangle, plotting to upend the patio;
the clothes line swings its noose,
pegs ready to pounce – a bucket
turns its back on me and the
crime I'm about to commit; hoe
in hand, I scrape. The filthy shawl
falls away. I've begged my spikes to
soften to silk, scrubbed the sap and
its sticky chaos, but a prickle is a
prickle and I am soiled to the bone.

MOULIN ROUGE

I sent my heart to the slaughterhouse,
but it ended up at the meatworks, the place
where scraps unfit for human consumption
go. The knacker's yard. Knowing men
in bloody overalls will peg me up
to their podium with all the other gristle
trophies, stripped back to the pink blush
of meat kept in line by the knife's edge.
A moulin rouge of frenzy, spinning poses of
panic in neat and naked rows, a salle
de spectacle that enthrals but not enough,
destined for the freezer, awaiting permission
to thaw. But then I changed my mind
about the whole putain de cabaret and
requested my heart be sent back first-class,
which it was, a little shaken and peg-grazed
but still intact, barely a bruise despite
its pirouettes. I'll pick away the sores
but I worry that once I start I won't be able to
stop like how maggots given half a chance
will chew their way through marrow until
all that's left is a string of holes only the wind
blows through.

DÉCOLLETÉ

If skin is supposed to hang neatly off the shoulders, snug as a summer blouse with room to breathe and barter, delicate as a décolleté (not to be confused with decollate which means 'to behead') then I think mine needs sending back. It has started to snag around the elbows and split; spindles poking through to tamper with the day, wire framework rusting in the sunlight. Sometimes these bones gallop at such a speed it's difficult to keep up. I've forgotten my skin on a train seat more than once, sized up by a stranger who smiles then hands it back, *mademoiselle?* I've left it slung across the back seat of a taxi, dumped at a soirée, in cloakrooms and countless métros but it's always sent straight back to my front door. This décalage between my bones and its business leaves me hors de soi: not quite here, not quite there, voyaging on an out of date passeporte, eyes like two moons shunted out of orbit, rolling back into their sockets to search for clues.

I wish I could shell myself: strip myself back to the fibrous husk I truly am, lift up the skull, scrape out the gunk, smear the walls for everyone to see, so that when beckoned back into myself, I might finally have reason to refuse.

se–décortiqué

se–décortiqué

A

'A' first reared its ox-head and two horns under the crack of a whip around 1800 BC in ancient Semitic ⨎ ploughing sense to the surface of the mind's muddy fields.

***

It took millennia for ⨎ to muster the courage to run away, still ⨎ became 'A' and my tongue – obediently waiting orders at the end of a lengthy chain – twists wildly in excitement.

***

Ah barely used t' no'ice 't, m' tongue, slumped 'neath a blank't a' spit an' short Yorkshuh vowels. *'D'y wan' owt from t' chippy?'* But then 't eight'een 't was ripped out, m' tongue, pinned t' whiteboard an' measured 'gainst those a' m' class.

***

A*AAAB. Hats off, young lady, welcome to Cambridge, your new abode. *Hinc lucem et pocula sacra.* How frightfully *infra dig* to read *lingua et litteris* anywhere else. Please, I pray, do *try* to make yourself feel at home.

***

Assessed on average saliva production, I scored higher than my peers: 1.5 litres a day as words retreated silently down my throat. But lagging behind in length, it was the English vowel span I couldn't master.

***

Together, m' tongue an' I, epiglottis t't tip, w' strained t' build a /p⊠⊠/ t'wards a better version a' m' self; stretching my [a] into /⊠:/ we pr/⊠:/cticed the eleg/⊠:/nt pirouettes of the prim/⊠:/ ballerin/⊠:/, performing the C/⊠:/mbridge edition of 'Oxford English' to /⊠:/ crowd that couldn't c/⊠:/re less.

But where are you *really* from?

***

We pulled many muscles trying to prove this skin a shawl, a layer of mud I could lose in the wash, beneath which a well-educated white girl would be keeping warm: a Kinder Surprise translated into human form ◯ |

***

It's not my tongue that lacks temper: intelligent domesticated beast, like the runway ox ⚡ 'ts sick t' back teeth a' pullin' carts whose cargo in't 'ts own.

B

The scaffolding for 'B' was first assembled around 4,000 years ago in Egypt as a hieroglyph signifying 'home' or ⊏⊐ 'shelter'.

***

Flip 'B' on its side and you can still make out the two
windows, but do not press your nose against the glass. I
tossed a stone through when language, rigid and reticent,
wouldn't bend with my tongue.

***

The vowels I stole were too bulky to speak or swallow.
They j/⊠:/mmed open my j/⊠:/w as if with sticks and like a
window stuck on a rusty latch for days I couldn't close.

***

Neighbours talked as neighbours do, so I prised the sticks
out // and papered over the cuts. The inside of my cheeks are
still so r/⊠:/w.

***

I know that language is no place for crime and disorder: it
should be a shelter not a shattering, but I can no longer call
this mouth my home.

***

So much has been replaced! Chandeliers ⊠ and chairs ⊠ and
doorknobs ⊠ and coffee tables ⊠ and lamps ⊠ and coatracks ⊠
and bookshelves ⊠… switched for the latest models.

***

I am tenant after tenant hauling in new furniture: curling
into the slick ⊠⊠⊠⊠ ⊠⊠⊠⊠ of the '⊠' only to fold into le fauteuil
crapaud of the 'ê'. This mouth is not my own.

***

What else can I do but pick up a pen, pitch a tent upon the
page and crawl inside? I've locked myself out, deeds and
documents prove nothing.

***

I peg down the punctuation then gather flint to make a fire, but my language will no longer light. It refuses to welcome these unlawful, thieving hands.

C

The first 'C' shape was carved in Phoenician and stood for a 'hunter's stick' or 'boomerang' ⌐. Hanging somewhere between a salute and a slump, its angle of inclination was adjusted by the Greeks and the Etruscans depending on the danger at hand ﹥. When thrown correctly, towards prey with purposeful spin, a boomerang whizzes horizontally and can strike a target dead. I try to do the same with my tongue, not so much to attack as to defend my place in the conversation, excuse the skin on my bones. But pivoting the point with rapid almost reckless spin, I lose my tongue in the /⊠r⊠⊠s/.

D

'D' first opened around 800 BC as a tent door flapping wildly in the wind ◁ The Greeks renamed it 'delta' Δ whilst the Romans tamed its unruly edges. As I whip out my Delta Sander 280W and set about sanding down a door that no longer fits its frame ⊠ I think about how my language rarely opens as smoothly as it should. I've been silent so long my jaw warps in its jamb. I'm left stranded on the wrong side of words: looking in ⊠ I think about ripping the door from its frame and building a better house, tearing my tongue from its throat and building a better body, but I can't master the tools to do justice to the task.

H

'H' was first erected in Egyptian hieroglyphics as a 'fence' or 'barrier' ▦ whose insurmountable boundary was built for keeping enemies out.

***

Later deemed a waste of natural resources, 'H' was disassembled from the alphabet in 500 A D when the danger was thought to have passed.

***

Sluggish an' sloppy 'anded, 'm 'appy to 'ear 'bout 'ow t' alphabet gorrid 'f its 'aitch; I 'ardly saw where y'd use it anyways, 'cept f' job int'views an' radio an' seminars an' stuff. But still ah'm sceptic an' got m' suspicions…

***

I've lived the barrier of language too long to think that enemies are always external: often, like this tongue, they grow and fester within.

***

[A]h cl[a]mbuh over't Yorkshuh vowels [a]h used t'know so well, dr[a]m[a]tisin' m' desp'r[a]te se[a]rch for s[a]fe [a]n' st[a]ble ground. But sn[a]ggin' 'pon their sh[a]rp wire edges, [a]m nor'[a]llowed t'come b[a]ck in.
***

Mistaken for enemy forces, I've fenced myself out my mouth and into a minefield. Each word I choose is an insult against the truth, and threatens to blow the cover on who I really am.

I
'I' was called 'yodh' in 1000 B C and grew from the Egyptian hieroglyph for an 'arm' or 'hand', , the palm of which, like my own, has always read a future of fatal entwinement.

***

As body and language, hand and hieroglyph, root and reroute
into each other, it's a silent painful love-affair that never ends
well.

***

My skeleton, like any other, is a place of scripture with death
scrawled into its walls. Each day its echo grows louder,
but even in the flesh, the spectacle of self-expression is a
mortifying task.

***

I am terrified of answering the phone: coughing up mud into
the ears of strangers. When it rings, I line my teeth up like
a dry stone wall † cheeks blaze in cremation † spit-roast my
tongue † whilst palms shovel pockets deep as graves.

***

My language grows a back bone the world seeks to break:
hear it crunch between my teeth if I clench down too hard.

z

Three-thousand years ago the Phoenicians carved out
the sharp double-edged tool of 'Z' in the name of 'zayin'
meaning 'axe'.

***

Hacked from a block of silence and measured up against a
lump of thought, 'Z' was hewed into shape by the Greeks
around 800 BC. Renamed 'zeta', it didn't meet the minimum
industry standard: the design fell short as language always
does.

***

My language is a work in progress rippled with shallow, parallel grooves: run a finger down the middle and you'll feel the cracks. Ask me a question and I'll chip away the words outside of what I really want to say. When all the unwanted marble is gone, you might almost understand.

*

JADE CUTTLE is Arts Commissioning Editor at *The Times*. Her criticism and reviews have been published in the *The Times*, *TLS*, the *Telegraph*, and the *Guardian*. She has been commissioned to write poetry for BBC Radio 3, BBC Contains Strong Language and the BBC Proms, winning competitions run by Ledbury Poetry Festival, the Poetry Society and Poetry Book Society. As a songwriter fusing metaphor with melody, Jade released an eco-themed album of poem-songs Algal Bloom through Warren Records with funding from the PRS foundation and Make Noise, performing across the BBC network and at festivals such as Latitude. Previously, she was a poetry editor at *Ambit*, worked at the Poetry Society and tutored at the Poetry School where she devised a poetry course for adults; judging the Costa Book Awards (both Poetry, and the Costa Book of the Year) and later the Gingko Prize alongside Simon Armitage. Her plant-whispering poetry workshops have been programmed at festivals, schools and universities and filmed for BBC One. She holds a first-class degree in Modern and Medieval Languages and Literature (Russian and French) from Cambridge University (Homerton College), and graduated with Distinction from the MA in Poetry at the University of East Anglia. (www.jadecuttle.com)

Trees feature very prominently in my work. I come back to them again and again. This has, I think, something to do with how I grew up: in a small village in central Jamaica called Coffee Grove. My grandmother, who raised me, was a farmer. Trees were all around. We often went to the yam ground, my grandmother's cultivation plot. When I think of my childhood, I see myself entering a deep woodland with cedars and logwood all around. I think that that landscape has deeply penetrated my imaginary.

There was also a lot of silence in my childhood. The pristine and clean, wholesome nature in which I grew up was a kind of protected kingdom that allowed me to listen to the sound of things. The muscular guango trees were like beings among whom we lived. To be attuned to nature is like having a kind of silence. You hear things more, you listen to things – to the world.

Now that I am grown and I live near a forest in Leeds, England, I am renewing my connection with that reality. Here, trees represent an alternative space, a refuge from an ultra-consumerist culture, from the increasingly alienating materialism of the society.

Thinking with Trees, my forthcoming collection with Carcanet Press, speaks to a primordial instinct of thinking with the elements, based on the idea that nature is a part of us. It is not just acted upon, but acts upon and with us. In my mind, there is a melting of the conceptual difference between the human and the tree, the rock, the mineral, etc. The poetry trains its graze on what links us with the elements. What interests me is process: the composition and decomposition of objects, the ecologies that work to keep us alive, even when we are unaware of them. Occasionally, I am privileged to have a deep sensation of process and I leap into those moments.

The observation of process is a political act linked to a reclamation of time. It highlights the fact that racism pushes us into an attitude of *always reacting*: to hurt, anger, provocation, exclusion. This is a theft of time, a robbery of the connection that we are meant to have, as humans, with *real* life. In that sense, these poems are an expression of my *taking time*, in a societal context that creates the environmental conditions that disproportionately rob Black lives of the benefits of time: leisure, relaxation, mental and physical well-being, etc.

Long timescales remind us of our connection to ancestry and to Earth, a world that exceeds us. Short timescales remind us of the need to be in the moment, to affirm the fullness of our human existence. 'Fallen Beech' imagines very long timescales that extend beyond human lifetimes, while 'On the First Day of Autumn' is more concerned with the sensual experience of the immediate present – the sounds and smells and feeling of the forest. Both long and short timescales push me to reckon with the environmental conditions currently affecting Black lives, they make ever present histories of exclusion from leisure in Black experience (the slave ship, the plantation, the tenement yard, the prison industrial complex).

In these poems and in the longer book (*Thinking with Trees*), poetry is a way of reclaiming time, a way of reasserting one's connection with the world. My personal history brings me to that political stance.

The use of gaps and spaces, as opposed to classic punctuation, is a visual enactment of the ruminative thinking that I am engaged in. It forces the reader to slow down, mirroring what we are supposed to be doing with nature – we can and should take our time with it.

*

CLIMBING TREES

These beeches are unclimbable
no furrows for feet

At home I knew a tree
by climbing it

Lost inside the guinep branches
I felt close to God

and I was hidden
in a place before birth

like a womb
nearing the sky

For hours I would imagine
I could turn into something else

one of those brown or green lizards
living up there.

The limbs of an old guinep tree
are suspended walkways

You travel with your belly
with your thighs   with all your feeling

The thick muscular limb is a road
you hug   your back is a caterpillar's

legs knowing
the skin of the tree

insteps rubbing
the green moss

Travelling above the earth
I go searching for something

that both tree and lizard have
the ability to see things down below

things that never see them
folks that never think they are seen

because they never learn
to see the world from trees

WALKING WITH THE WORD 'TREE'

To have money
is to have time
To have time
is to have the forests
and the trees

I look at my baby
mindsliding
in the sticky
film of the bud
rubbing her thoughts
between
fingers

and knowing the
purple lips of the
involucres in her mouth

And me   am I living
my childhood all over
again?

For her a wood will not be
    burned for fire coal
    where the pig pen is
    where you hide from your Mama
    where you escape from scolding & rolling eyes
    where the duppies live
    where the madman lives
    where wild animals stray dogs
    and the unwanted go to die

And me   am I living
my childhood all over
again?

a child's way
of pinching flowers
a child's way of touching buds
but what I had never known
this way of listening to the forest

Did Daisy
Miss Patsy's eleventh child
and my playmate
even know her name
was a flower?

In Porus life was un-
pastoral
The woodland was there
not for living in   going for walks
or thinking
Trees were answers to our needs
not objects of desire
woodfire

Catch butterflies
along the way to grandmother
on the other side of the yam field
Just don't do something foolish
like lose the money or
take too long
so the pot don't cook
before daddy reach home

There's a way of paying attention to plants
a way of listening to trees
a way to hold a flower in your hand
now that I'm here in a park in England

and I stop when called by the pistils of a tree
There is something in the pink
that speaks so clearly to me   saying
glad you stopped   I saw you
from far away

I don't even know
what *they* call it
but I want to know
what it tells me
about itself

its appearance
with thousands of others
on this tree
that up to April
seemed like death

Our parents and grandparents planted yams
potato slips   reaped tomatoes
carrots and so on
Then market then money
then food then clothes
then shoes to go to school

Now I'm practising a different way
of being with the woods   only
I try not to stray too far from the path...

The daisies glitter
at my feet

AUTUMN

I enter
peel off the skin of my living room
It is October
and the light that falls
on the leaves
rises again
in a swell
while the red floor of the woodland
stretches like an avenue
through high maples and oaks
My feet press down into
the leaves and I wonder

how many seasons lie here beneath my feet
Here there is no enclosure
only cells
making sounds on a frequency so low in
a world distant
from words
unpossessed and full

ROOTS

summer's day in quartz
ships' smooth skin on water
broad beach of volcanic sores
a thousand selves
and more

around me the rocks are
petrified alligators
gorgeous in black blisters

they butt the wind
as if they could move again
and pounce with the tide

I watch their swift running
from among the dunes
and listen to the waves
rustle the leaves of stone

to my right the silver sand sings
a lone seaside pine on a butte
blooms into a parasol
my heart is a jumble of rocks

inside there are so many creatures
so many seas
are those reptiles running
another time moving
are the rocks a sea within a sea

I will sleep in the sand
in the rocks and the quartz that oozes
like sores from the skin of granite

the silver sand sinks and
I do not know how far I will go
and the rocks and the sea sing
about a time that is within
not mine   in a voice too low

to my right the tropical sunshine
and the lone seaside pine
surrounded by the smouldering wicks
of rock samphire   I have run to be here
far from home

the rain stings   it is cold
my knees burn from clumps of fescue
as I kneel looking out to sea

Can we not from this height
hear ten volcanoes
spitting their lava to create the islands
and beside it we have a place to live
in god's dust
I want to know more
about the roots that nourish the rocks
that keep them tall and flourishing

DAFFODILS
(SPECULATION ON FUTURE BLACKNESS)

It's time to write about daffodils
again
to hear a different sound
from the word

daffodil

Imagine daffodils in the corner
of a sound system
in Clapham

Can't you?
Well you must

try to imagine daffodils
in the hands of a black family

on a black walk
in spring

ALL TOO HUMAN

A grey squirrel appears
under a beech sapling
smells its way closer
   In the matted spikenard
I am not threatening   it seems
the squirrel could almost
come to my feet
except

it catches my
   too human gaze
so shifts course
   goes off a different way
   and as it goes
every controlled unspooling of the limbs
is a tenderness drawn inside me
   a blanket of silk
the spell of its camber
disappearing into plush mounds of litterfall

*

JASON ALLEN-PAISANT is a Jamaican poet who lives in Leeds. His creative writing (poetry, memoir, critical life writing) addresses issues of time, race, class, and the environmental conditions underpinning Black identity. His poetry has been featured or is forthcoming in *Granta*, *PN Review*, *Callaloo*, BBC Radio 3's *The Verb*, *Stand* and other venues. His first full-length book of poems is entitled *Thinking with Trees*. His other non-fiction projects include a book of personal essays titled *Reclaiming Time.* Jason is a Lecturer in Caribbean Poetry and Decolonial Thought, with joint appointments in the School of English and the School of Languages, Cultures and Societies at the University of Leeds, where he is also director of the Institute for Colonial and Postcolonial Studies.

I'm standing in an open field, throwing a tennis ball as far as I can towards the spring-equinox clouds that keep changing, turning to rain. Playing with and against motion – sometimes I think that this is the main thing I do when working on a poem. The poem becomes a ball that I toss up into the air, trying to keep it hovering, moving forward and further. Or perhaps I'm trying to turn the poem into an engine, so that at some elusive, unpredictable point I'd be able to let it take off. Reading the *Philosophical Investigations*, I've found it fascinating that Wittgenstein links meaning to motion:

> 'When one means something, it is oneself that means'; so one sets oneself in motion. One rushes ahead, and so cannot also observe one's rushing ahead. Indeed not. (*Philosophical Investigation*, 456)

The process of working on a poem often feels to me like that of getting lost. I am unable to observe myself, because while trying to create a poem in motion, I am, in fact, in a state of motion too. Fortunately, poetry lends itself effortlessly to motion. Even the way we write poems – vertically, from top to bottom, unconsciously echoing the law of gravity – evokes movement. I remember, aged nine, learning how to throw a basketball – you should shoot it forward and at the same time make sure the ball backspins all the way through. To me, this duality of movement reflects the flow of a poem: the text moves in one direction, while the enjambments create backspins that turn it into a spiralling-continuous motion, forming a sense of suspense by going against the end of the sentences, against any sense of pause.

Perhaps all this time I've been trying to create moving sculptures instead of poems. It is as if I've been carving line breaks in the soft stone of the script, leading myself and a possible reader in circles around the text that turns into a spiralling slide, where each spiral offers a slight change of direction or meaning or, hopefully, both.

The act of throwing a poem like a ball is an act of communication: someone is hopefully waiting at the other end of the field to catch this spiralling wave of a poem. To me, Wittgenstein's notion of meaning as *setting oneself in motion* explains why an assumed audience is an integral part of the creative process: 'Yes, meaning something is like going towards someone' (PI, 457).

As a reader I hold onto poems that resist resolutions, poems that keep moving, spinning, changing their minds. Earlier in the Investigation, Wittgenstein proposes that it is not the business of philosophy to resolve contradictions and I often think it is the same for poetry:

> It is not the business of philosophy to resolve a contradiction by means of a mathematical or logico-mathematical discovery, but to render surveyable the state of mathematics that troubles us – the state of affairs *before* the contradiction is resolved. (PI, 125)

For my own practice of poetry writing I choose to read it like this: *It is not the business of* poetry *to resolve a contradiction…* And yet if a poem resists resolution, how do you – the writer – know when it is complete? Presumably it could go on and on. Here is a possible answer – imagine the poem as a small creature: it has to be complete so that you'd be able to hold it in your palms without the risk of its parts – limbs, eyes – falling apart. And at the same time, because this poem-creature is complete, it can now use its limbs and eyes – and so it keeps moving, wriggling, trying and hopefully managing to escape from your palms, going towards someone.

*

NEW YORK, I'VE FALLEN

for your absence of blue, an element –
locked, like a star. How did it happen, halfway
through the queue, that I started
to cry? There must be a trilogy
that begins with a rose
and ends with a streetlight – a blue
dot in the snow – deceptive
like water: clear and seemingly seeking
a deeper conclusion. I would never
have given you ten out of
twenty, except at that night
when the guy at the bus stop started – *hey,*
what's your favourite place? And I noticed
the rain, the way it was fractured the second
it hit the blue lights – the tour de force
start of November. New York,
it was then when I knew it had always
been people like us – who grew up in small
places – who know nothing is worse
than the clear-porcelain moon
of blue sky, who'd go for the streetlights
reflections in quicksilver rain – any time – yes,
give me winter's exaggerated
romanticism – a bitten-pink rose
in cigarette glass. I have fallen for each
fissure of pavement, for the crowd altering
the shape of quick
seconds, for the postman holding a pink
envelope – that wonder of physically
carrying a small piece of writing
from one place to another through snow and blue
snow. New York, that I'm writing you

here, in Monmouth café off Borough street,
London – lol –
what do I know of the light falling
backwards past Brooklyn Bridge. It's early
July and the waitress feels sorry
for me – I can tell. Perhaps it's the way
I'm holding onto the purple-blue leaf
in my bracelet as if I am trying to track down
my pulse. What do I know
of the heavy sleet turning to snow
in a city I visited once, for three
nights. Here, the Thames turning inwards, the air –
heavy with summer and impossible
heat. What do I know of the dreamers
fighting a blue-upturned umbrella
next to the Guggenheim trees, of the girl
running with a yellow guitar on her back, crying
into her phone: *where? I can't hear you –*,
of the way her breath changes with each leaf
of snow, of the man at the bus stop, calling
through fast-moving sleet and blue
smoke: *you, my pal*
for the night – what are the odds
you're into the greatest
espresso? What do I know of the yellow-plum
trees encircling a crescent
that until recently never really, particularly
mattered, of the local café
where the owner has broken
her arm and her fiancée's car and her promise
to place a blue rose every morning
on the windowsill snow until
her grief passes, or at least changes
light, or at least let her fall

asleep in the night, of the game-changing
headline across the Atlantic, declaring
her place *c'est Un Must*, of the entire
neighbourhood's extraordinary something
of a renaissance, of the pink
envelope she opens and opens and
fires like a paper-plane into
the snow. There must be
a trilogy, where three-quarters through, you
stand in a five-hour queue
with a guy who's unlocking blue smoke
under flickering lights, who is out of his
element – and sure, so are you – yet you totally
know what he means when he says he is hoping
the coffee will live up to the hype.

I'M LETTING VELÁZQUEZ*

come up with the questions.
Does the absence of blue

resonate with the sound of imminent
rain? Is the extraordinary

yellow a tad too
rebellious for the sole illustration

of yolk as a symbol
of how easy it is – to draw

one's attention, to mistake
every circular shape for the chance

of a moon?
Things are holding together

quite well and are going
to break any

second – I reckon – but I'm letting
Velázquez come to terms

with the non-accidental theatrical
darkness around the impeccable

setting of spotlights –
the two central figures, the knife turning

the plate into a compass,
the spoon

almost touching the burning-clay pan,
the circle-in-circle

of the brass vessel, just
leaning under the boiling-oil centre

of drama and
light. Here's the palm

holding an egg
as if holding the shaping in progress

of a non-elegant
thought. Here's the boy

carrying what must be
the heaviest

moon but I know Velázquez
would say I'm going

too far.
He'd say I forgot

to give the two characters 'space –' let them
be there and

not there.
Each to their own

world of intentions and unanswered
calls,

each to their own constellations
of arbitrary objects floating

from one wall to another like an empirical
study in darkness and

play.
If you tell me

a story – he'd say –
how the glass bottle goes

with the way he's avoiding
her eyes,

or how the red terracotta
brings the light into

action until everything falls
into places – I'm

out.
So I'm letting the sounds

own the space
for a while: the wine poured into

a goblet, the door opened and
closed like a possible

action on hold.
Then he comes back, puts his hat

on the table.
No, he says, only

kidding. It's seriously raining
out there.

After Diego Velázquez, Old Woman Cooking Eggs

THE CITY

Summer solstice (first scene). A girl with a knife cuts a pear
in half. Think 'Venus Rising from the Sea' goes city
and smoke. At the bar, a man dreams a glass of champagne
like an unbalanced thought. Think 'Streetcar' goes 'Gatsby', the scene
with the boat. She lights a cigarette as if it's made of thin glass,
he's telling a story as if it's a city uncut. Cut.

A nightmare. The girl shouts in a black-and-white dream. Cut.
There's a gallery. Think MOMA but rough. She looks at a pear
made of bronze, in a nest of cast iron and glass.
The gallery turns into a field of white roses, a white city,
is it still June? Think Fellini's dancing scene
in '8½.' One hand's filling a glass with champagne

the other offering the glass. *Champagne?*
The girl dances and dances. Think Matisse, 'The Cut-Outs'. Cut.
Close-ups: Scissors. A dancer. Another dream scene.
Think 'Last Year at Marienbad', the moon like a pear –
the shape of a question. The actors arrive at an improvised city,
think musical setting, the sky made of turquoise-stained glass.

London. A waitress with eyes like stained glass.
Think Soho stilettos, fake mascara, cheap champagne.
The phone rings with a 'Moon River' cover. Think New York City
at the end of the line. *Can you hear me? We've met at the –*. Cut
to a mirror. Think Manet's 'A Bar at the Folies-Bergère'. Cerulean pear
made of a girl and a corset too tight. But next, it's the girl with the scene-

stealing smile. Ready? It's 'The Perfect Summer' deleted scene:
a lake, pink lemonade, a girl's wearing soft tan. Think 'The Glass
Menagerie', anything but. Sunglasses like a Venetian mask, a spiral pear-
and-amaretto tart, she drinks too much champagne
then hides and throws up. Think 'Manhattan', the outtakes. Cut.
Rome. A girl opens an envelope with the tip of a knife. Think 'La Città

e la Casa', pages revealing city by city as if every city
is cut into rivers and sliced into streets down to the seeds of each scene.
The phone rings. *Don't hang up*. She hangs up. Cut.
Later, she watches how sand travels like rain inside hourglass
bulbs as if it's a low-budget film. Sound effects: rain, champagne
flute drops from a hand. Somewhere a girl wears a ring like a pear

on a knife, like the deepest of cuts. Somewhere a city
is closed and is endless, is the shape of an 8, a pear mise-en-scène
where a glass stem is held like a spine and a promise. *Champagne?*

AFTER-PARTY

Yes, there was the abundance of nightfall –
the sky with a parachute scar,
the spoon clinking

on glass.
But no one could trace, like a hymn,
the blue-vanishing

trail of an apple-throw
arc. Things like this
happen –

a hula-hoop pivoting
beauty, a wonder thrown
like a firework into

the crowd.
Some say it was only
an arrow, meaning –

an error.
Others swear they could hunt down
the deepest

of sighs.
That the transformation
from an apple into

a question
was inevitable –
that the answer was no more

than a boy
offsetting fire with sci-fi
animation – I mean – what

would you choose?
The possession of Europe and
Asia / the greatest of warriors' rivers

and tongues – the green in their night-vision
maps / a doorbell and how it rings
night.

ANOTHER CITY

The way you ran into the last rush-hour of the morning,
like a character in one of Sempé's city sketches,

with your coat collapsing and the wind
not helping, water-coloured by the racing cars and rain,

which wasn't even falling enough
to cause such a storm. There's a picture, or a place,

where everyone's thrown in their city's steps and hours,
walking or smoking into each other,

holding their phones, *T'es où? Allô, t'es où?*
On the corner of

Baker Street and Marylebone, I think I was
the only one not moving, holding onto my mobile, to all my

where-are-you texts and messages, so I'd look busy
and not lost.

ET TU?

Tu as dit sérieusement, sans distance, sans un soupçon d'ironie,
le mot 'déconstruction,' toi, mon ami.

Yasmina Reza, 'Art'

Look closer, here is the water
we dream. Your eye for a comic-strip

ocean, my weakness
for rain-following

streets. Look
closer – I'm always the writer

test driving the sky with no
moon – a yellow plum

by the fire, a boy
checking himself out

in a curved-mirror
spoon. So tonight, let me drive you

into my own, compositional
weather – shall we

balance a glass
on the unstable dream

of a table?
Are you with me –

my friend?
Have you got the wrong

message? It happened
to me a few seconds

ago, and last week
during 'Art' of all plays – of all

places –
when I had to look

for the things we call
keys. Language is all we are

left with –
I thought, holding on tight

to the missing back
of my seat.

IN THE STUDIO

1   *I wanted to do all this*

to flatten a bead to a disc – a leaf of sea
glass, to find the blue of a rose
in the quick of my wrist, to catalogue
every streetlight, each impossible rumour, the silver
of trees, to circle the city – my pulse in my palm
like a spring. Was the night open
to that possibility – the sky, an equation
of stars versus full-hearted
rain? I wanted to test how a gesture
turns into a physical land – an amplified
thought, how it changes when connected
to sound or joined to a sketch of blue
light, I wanted to watch how a lightbulb ends up
standing for light.

2   *That night the city was unapologetically*

there: a finally, fully
developed concept of streetlights and
rain. When the bridges took off
in a great-pelican flight – entrusting the river
to us – I gave names to each applicant:
the tracing-pink glass, the girl with a penchant
for imperatives, the band at The Drunk Anarchist

trying out turn-of-the-century
jazz and blue smoke. Poet, remember, your material
is words. Was the night cerulean, cold and
misleading? Was the city that different to the one
you had left with a friend? I now understand
what I thought I couldn't: the place where
I'm confident is here.

3   *The flight of plates*

didn't happen at once or according to plan.
When the spoons lifted their wings with a cry
of miniature birds, heading north and then
south, trying out clicks of clear silver, the seashore
became endless with rain, the blue-heron wings
didn't make any sense but the rebelling sound
of the air – compressed and released like a girl
who would not play this game. I think she said dreams
matter. I think she said that's Okay to not
understand. I lifted the near-miss of a moon
with one hand. The sunset not setting I couldn't
explain. Mistakes always happen, she said. In fact, it is strange
when they don't, she concluded, brushing sea glass
and salt off my hair.

IT IS IN LANGUAGE THAT AN EXPECTATION*

Perhaps you wanted to test out a story
so you went to the balcony and constructed an airplane
out of telephone wires, a small fire, a sketch of a city
you wanted to fly as a high-altitude kite in the unsettled
weather, so you turned it into an engine, a poem
made of paper-plane wings. There are so many countries
that lead away from your balcony, a tennis ball flowering, spinning
away from the quick of your fist towards a distant-blue
circle, your pulse like a risk-taking rumour
in the long-summer evening you play on-repeat –
the street in the mirror, the moon taking shape in the room
of your script, and outside – like a study in streetlights
and rain – the city you live in and still can't afford
after so many years. But perhaps that particular 'so many
years –' if anything, gave you this small insight
to hold onto, try and release: that your own
concept of time links to that

---

* 'It is in a language that an expectation and its fulfilment make contact.'
  – Wittgenstein, *Philosophical Investigation*, # 445

of suspense. Somewhere, a probability –
high as the gate of a story – the one you mistake
for a place – begins to take shape: the throw of a ball
like a long-distance question, your own misconception
expanding, echoing a city you leave
and keep coming back to as if in a dream, except
this time you know you're running this dream: the balcony
takes off like a light-flying machine, the moon pulling the script
of your street as short film, the night ringing the citadel sky
like a copper-blue bell in a country you're still trying
to get, your hand raising a glass to the first
day of spring as if you have always held onto nothing
but this – the glass an exception – *that an expectation* –
a yellow ball spiralling towards an improvised
land – *and its fulfilment* – the fall or the poem you're carrying
as if you were trying to catch it or give it a name –
make contact.

CIRCLES

Loss has a wider choice of directions
Than the other thing.

W.S. Merwin, *The Nails*

Now, as the rain turns into
sketches of rain, a girl draws a circle
on the quick-yellow sand.

In the picture, the sea is another
quick second. Hours are physical
matters, thinks the man who quit smoking

two hours ago –
in the picture. Here, he doesn't fall
into his palms, he doesn't seem

absent. Throw a pebble
into the water and watch how the circles
get bigger, thinks the woman

outside the picture, watching the snow
taking hold of a city she now
calls home.

Click

Two glasses of water waiting to happen.
Two dragonflies, blue and
quick-blue.

I wouldn't mind being that kind of adventurous,
thinks the woman watching the street
holding onto the snow.

I wouldn't mind being that kind of pretty,
thinks the child watching a bee
fighting a pond. Throw a pebble into the water

and go for a walk.
In the picture, the rain never stops
or begins, the man doesn't fly

out of the streetlights, the city,
that year. In the picture – that year
never happened.

Click

A child, cutting the sea out of blue and dark
paper. A hot-air balloon in a short
animation. A telescope catches

a moon.
I wouldn't mind being that kind of lost,
thinks the tree watching a car in the rain,

thinks the pond watching the door
open and close, thinks the picture taken
again of a circle turning

into a hole,
thinks the child drawing a rainstorm
before it takes form:

a tree practicing being a tree. A sandcastle
made out of water. Throw a pebble into the picture
and watch.

I'M BACK IN THE RECORDING STUDIO

I'm back in the recording studio –
testing salt against

choice.
On your left-hand side – a city grows out

of a river. On your right-hand side –
I thought

we were going home but instead
there are trees of blue-green, a paper-boat

map. I'm back
in the recording studio – testing smoke

against glass.
If you look back – my sister

waving her hand. A carousel spinning
into an ammonite shell.

Nobody's shouting *Where are you going?*
It's not that.

*

Now that you dive into three different languages, you're –
the mouth of a river / a ship

of three masts / the gorgons running in six
directions. Backward and forward and

backward.
I thought we were going home – but instead we're going

home. I'm here
at the recording studio – testing dream

against light.
On your right-hand side – a door. On your left-hand side –

a shout. Now that you swear
in multiple

tongues –
now that you're back.

Nobody's saying *Why are you crying?*
It's not that.

*

STAV POLEG's poetry has been published on both sides of the Atlantic, including in *The New Yorker*, *Kenyon Review*, *Poetry London*, *Poetry Ireland Review* and *PN Review*. She regularly collaborates with fellow artists and poets. Her graphic-novel installation, *Dear Penelope: Variations on an August Morning*, created with artist Laura Gressani, was acquired by the Scottish National Gallery of Modern Art. Her pamphlet, *Lights, Camera,* was published in 2017 by Eyewear. Her theatre work was read at the Traverse Theatre, Edinburgh, and the Shunt Vaults, London, and most recently at Kettle's Yard gallery, Cambridge. She serves on the editorial board of *Magma Poetry* and has recently facilitated collaborative work between poets and filmmakers for the magazine. She teaches for the Poetry School, London.

My poetry recalls and records the events in the lives of women in Afghanistan. My poems bear witness to the experiences of women I knew and speak to their bravery and accomplishments – all unacknowledged till now. My poems also capture stories I was told as a child, stories that contained lessons for a young Afghan girl.

More specifically, my poetry tries to capture those moments when a woman tries to justify herself and her acts by telling her side of the story. I have tried to tell their stories in the most unjudgmental way possible to an audience with the hope that my audience will understand the injustices experienced by women in Afghanistan. The women of my poems are strong women. I have learned so much from them, and I benefited from their example, wisdom and courage. They helped me become a woman of restless mind and a strong heart. These poems are dedicated to them.

Storytelling has a long tradition in Afghan culture. Stories are passed down orally. Every woman even or especially those who are illiterate knows and has memorized a few important stories – to share in order to enhance the listeners' wisdom and to teach one to take life for its hardship as well as its good times. I grew up among women who never went to school – my grandmothers, my mother, my aunts. Their philosophy of life has always been, 'in the face of hardship, patience is remedy'. When I embarked on my journey to become more educated, I began to reflect on the lives of the women I have always admired. I began to question my admiration for them. They were suffering and yet they accepted it. I became critical of their patience. And inevitably, with more and more education, patience became elusive and did not stay with me. Instead, I found the courage and the space to pick up a pen and write poems that say the unsaid and name the unnamed.

These poems are also more than just stories. Oscillating between poetic images in Persian and ideas formulated in English, I also practice this art of translation at the level of emotion and imagination. A poet like myself thinks in one language and measures and understands experiences with a different language. And it was learning English that gave me my voice as a poet, enabling me to distance myself as well as to comprehend the connection with the tradition I was brought up in. With this force of language, I found myself crafting poetry that spoke of the particular experiences of Afghan women in the most honest and serious way, one that somehow encompasses universality. In hindsight, the poems came from memories and served to commemorate and acknowledge.

One of the challenges in writing these poems has been the crucial act of understanding my own feelings about these stories, especially the ones that involve familial narratives. In the process of writing, I question myself. I doubt myself, and yet I become certain when the poem is finished. The ending to each one of these poems is a reconciliation with the self that I have become, through questions, search, reflection and development. That encompassing 'self' is the storyteller and the voice in these poems, who is also the person I am today.

*

FORTY NAMES

I

Zib was young.
Her youth was all she cared for.
These mountains were her cots
The wind her wings, and those pebbles were her friends.
Their clay hut, a hut for all the eight women,
And her Father, a shepherd.

He knew every cave and all possible ponds.
He took her to herd with him,
As the youngest daughter
Zib marched with her father.
She learnt the ways to the caves and the ponds.

Young women gathered there for water, the young
Girls with the bright dresses, their green
Eyes were the muses.

Behind those mountains
She dug a deep hole,
Storing a pile of pebbles.

II

The daffodils
Never grew here before,
But what is this yellow sea up high on the hills?

A line of some blue wildflowers.
In a lane toward the pile of tumbleweeds
All the houses for the cicadas,
All your neighbors.
And the eagle roars in the distance,
Have you met them yet?

The sky above through the opaque skin of
Your dust carries whims from the mountains,
It brings me a story.
The story of forty young bodies.

III
A knock,
Father opened the door,
There stood the fathers,
The mothers' faces startled.
All the daughters standing behind them
In the pit of dark night,
Their yellow and turquoise colors
Lining the sky.

'Zibon, my daughter,
Take them to the cave.'
She was handed a lantern
She took the way.
Behind her a herd of colors flowing.
The night was slow,
The sound of their footsteps a solo music of a mystic.

Names:
Sediqa, Hakima, Roqia,
Firoza, Lilia, Soghra.
Shah Bakhat, Shah Dokht, Zamaroot,
Naznin, Gul Badan, Fatima, Fariba.
Sharifa, Marifa, Zinab, Fakhria, Shahparak, MahGol,
Latifa, Shukria, Khadija, Taj Begum, Kubra, Yaqoot,
Nadia, Zahra, Shima, Khadija, Farkhunda, Halima, Mahrokh, Nigina,
Maryam, Zarin, Zara, Zari, Zamin,
Zarina,

At last Zibon.

I V
No news. Neither drums nor flutes of
Shepherds reached them, they
Remained in the cave. Were
People gone?

Once in every night, an exhausting
Tear dropped – heard from someone's mouth,
A whim. A total silence again

Zib calmed them. Each daughter
Crawled under her veil,
Slowly the last throbs from the mill-house

Also died.
No throbbing. No pond. No nights.
Silence became an exhausting noise.

V

Zib led the daughters to the mountains.

The view of the thrashing horses, the brown uniforms
All puzzled them. Imagined
The men snatching their skirts, they feared.

We will all meet in paradise,
With our honored faces
Angels will greet us.

A wave of colors dived behind the mountains,
Freedom was sought in their veils, their colors
Flew with wind. Their bodies freed and slowly hit

The mountains. One by one, they rested. Women
Figures covered the other side of the mountains,
Hairs tugged. Heads stilled. Their arms curved
Beside their twisted legs.

These mountains became their cots
The wind their wings, and those pebbles their friends.
Their rocky cave, a cave for all the forty women,
And their fathers and mothers disappeared.

A SURVIVAL PRAYER

1

Those summer nights in Kabul, tranquility
Was in the orchard of apricot trees:
In their images and shadows.
What happened to Uncle Najib?
What happened to the neighboring apple trees?

The nights are unknown,
The mornings are disturbed by the darkness,
Wake me up, father.
This is not the city
I live in. Neither is that one
My city, which I have called mine.

2

A long river flowing exhausted
Across the spring season,
A stream of coal-filled rocks.
It flows, flows,
Hitting the shores, where the tulips are born with thorns.
Though my mother says:
The tulips' petals are the praying hands of a woman.

The tulips are frozen deep down
Under the river,
I feel cold over my hands,
Cover me, mother.
This is not the nature
I was born with. Neither is it in my nature,
To survive this river.

3
I pray to the clouds
For rain.
Instead, the sound of shootings,
Some men scream,
Into the night.
The sound reaches my ears so fast,
I feel mortal again.
Hold my hands, brother. If there is a war again,
I will not pray for peace. Nor will I call it a war.

MY GRANDMOTHER'S RUBY RING

My grandmother wears a deep red ring,
A ruby set into a silver plate.

She lived in the valleys.
An orphan girl, herding her sheep in the fields.
A virgin: not yet menstruating, she became the bride
For another orphan. A ring was given to her
In a man's name, she was taken away.

She became a wife and lived in the city,
Caring for the man, his four brothers
His four sisters and their sad stories.

Seasons passed by, hardships:
She was separated from her husband
And went to live with her three boys and their families.

Throughout her separation,
She had always dreamed about her husband sitting
Under the shade of the apricot trees, or watering the
Tomato plants in the garden – she was *Zulaykha*
and He *Yosuf* – she always referred to him
As the prophet in her dreams.

She does not complain about the wounds on her hands.
A mother in law, a grandmother,
And gradually she became
A great-grandmother.
She had never shed a tear over the shattering clay-roofs
Under the snowfalls.

Now her story is about an old woman waiting for death.
The ring goes to the one who washes her body.
Only the woman who washes her well, dresses her properly and
Pays respect to her body will inherit her ring.

IN SEARCH OF A WOMAN

1

As *morning* melody breaks,
This city breathes in the middle of some dried dust.
Street vendors start by the river
Selling all kind of drugs for the city.

This opaque people
Smoking hashish.

Its once inky blue river, twisted through the city,
It is now a broken river –
Its banks darkened by trash of all kinds.

2

Once, after *midday* prayers,
Women headed to the city's river
To wash their clothes, rubbing and pounding them
On its stones, crossing the blue carpet of the river
Above was the turquoise water,
A mirror, an immortal soul of the city.

3

Now after midday,
This riverbank is home for this opaque people.
As the *Mughreb* sunset fades out,
These men head to the mosques.

4

I search in the streets of Kabul for a woman.
Instead of writing poetry,
I search for her, inside and outside of each room.
Where could she be at this time of the day?

5
Kabul then sleeps.
From the window of my house, I remain
In a room filled with women and children.

The odor of their clothes, the smell of the children,
Over and over, the door is locked.
Looking for a transcendence to emerge,
Or a memory to reside, each day is the same day.
I continue to write a poem.

DURRANI

One red autumn evening, she came to our village.
'She is a wolf,' men said, grabbing their shotguns,
'She is a fox,' women said, rushing toward their chicken-huts.

Through the window, I could see
the centuries-old graveyard,
that night someone had left two candles lit.

'The wolves have come to our village, we need to hurry,'
A hand pulled me away from the window.

Everyone sat together,
reciting *Surahs* from the Quran.
I sat next to my mother, in anticipation.

Mothers put their children to bed.
Men sat with shotguns resting on their arm.
I refused to sleep, watching from the window.

Then a song came from between
the watermelon grounds and the apricot trees,
I hurried back to the window.

There I saw a woman.
Her wrinkled Chador had fallen off her shoulders,
her face illuminated by the candle light.

She walked toward me, close enough so I could see
the motion of her feet beneath her dress.
She sang and laughed. Then she disappeared.

Years later, remembering that night, I asked my mother,
'Who was this woman who sang me poetry',
With cadences that captivated me.

She was *Durani*, my mother said.
A Pashtun woman, who dishonored her family.
by falling in love with a Hazara man from our village.

At night she found solace in our village, but only nights,
lit by candles left in the cemetery.
By her forbidden love.

KABUL IN A HAIKU

1

Summer evening in Kabul –
dust fills the valleys
the trees stay tranquil.

Autumn rains –
the almond trees' flowers fall –
broken.

All streets wrapped with
hoarfrost, I don't see an
old man walking.

Deep down – the colorful little flowers
sprout in spring.

2

From behind the window –
the moon is edged
        among the grapevines.

Early morning on the wet muddy streets,
an old man pushes a carriage –
    full of yellow mangoes.

The midday sun –
the workers lean on
    the trunk of the blackberry trees.

In twilight, beside the dried river of Kabul –
only the gale walks
on the streets.

3
With the summer rains,
the neighbor's clay-wall
melts.

By the end of autumn,
the grapes are well ripened, the bees
are satisfied.

With a peep of the sunrise,
the snow disappears over the clay-huts.

In spring,
the old man adds more clay on the roofs.

4
The summer stream of
Qarabaqh village
flows over pebbles and plants.

The fish congregate in the opening
of the stream in autumn –
blue and white.

The window frames are under frost –
yet the stream still flows.

In spring, the little girls
wash their dishes in the stream –
their noises falling in the air.

5
At midnight in my village –
a white wolf whimpers in our kitchen.

The smell of fresh baked bread
makes me feel kinder.

Midday,
mother walks with me to the wheat farms.

Dinner is served in a bowl –
two women and three kids, sit to eat.

Five people crawl under one quilt –
soft and warm- the moon beams behind the windows.

QUARANTINE

In the slowest pace of the unknown times
My father's hand caresses his headless cellphone.
He wakes me to tell me.
Times are uncertain. The legless virus is deadly.

His words in the invisible wire reach me
In between love and worry.
In summary, he says.
Take care of yourself.

Through the sunless sky his flawless voice echoes
Clear memories from wartime.
Stuck in the basement,
A father and his daughter are laying, foreheads on the ground.

My arms fall restful on the chair,
Or perhaps they are losing their
Pleasure of pain to numbness –
Like raw salmon served cold.

The only visitor from home comes in its best attire,
The moon in ivory color.
I appeal. I pray.
At least the pregnant Venus should change its color. Perhaps to red.

The night does not listen to me,
Nor to the owl that has taken up a room
On my bed.
It too is worried in its stuffed skin.

The longer the night gets,
The less superior the moon,
I, and the owl become.
The only visible color is the color of dark against the dark.

The veins on my wrests are now vessels with throbbing, as if they
Are listening to my heartbeats from behind my ears.
My sleepy hands are changing shapes.
Neither claws nor paws.

The soles of my feet are rupturing.
I feel the invisible water
Flowing in circles.
Four continents map the entirety of my body.

I am either an earless star,
Or some mud-dirt soon to meet the water,
I find ways to re-think about the situation.
I re-congregate my brothers and sisters,

My mother and my father,
From the far, far corners of the world.
I am the tongue. The other, the ear.
The other, the mouth.

The other, the eye.
The other, the neck.
The others, the heart, the brain,
The right arm, the left, the right leg, the left.

Like an ocean we swim to one another,
Back into lands. As members, we meet again.
One by one we are wholesome again.
In fall, in rise, in rise, in fall.

Like a gentle touch, like a slow heartbeat in the moment,
I blow a kiss.
I tell him, grapes will be sweeter in September,
And we will go to north of Kabul with my sisters and brothers.

27 April 2020

*

PARWANA FAYYAZ was born in Kabul, Afghanistan in 1990. From the age of seven to sixteen, she was raised in Quetta, Pakistan. After finishing high school in Kabul, she enrolled in an English language immersion program and subsequently began her undergraduate studies in Chittagong, Bangladesh. She transferred to Stanford University and earned both her B.A. in 2015, with a major in Comparative Literature (with Honors) and a minor in Creative Writing (Poetry) under the supervision of late Eavan Boland, and her M.A. in Religious Studies in 2016. She moved to Cambridge University to pursue a PhD in Persian Studies at Trinity College in September of 2016 and completed a thesis titled, *Poetry and Poetics: the Sufi Eye and the Neoplatonic Vision in Jāmī's Salāmān va Absāl*, in 2020. She took up Junior Research Fellowship as the Carmen Blacker Fellow at Peterhouse, Cambridge University in October 2020.

Parwana divides her time between pursuing research on medieval Persian poetry and writing her own poetry. She is currently working on her first collection of poems and writing a monograph based on her PhD dissertation.

I've always felt the past to be close. At times as a sort of companionship, as in the case of the dead, but at others a remorse that we can't, as much as we sometimes might want to, return to people and places that are gone. The idea of a 'true' past, in which life continues on as it once did, seems only to exist in the sort of place Wallace Stevens once described as 'remote lands' where 'what is dead lives with an intensity beyond any experience of life'. It is a different past that concerns these poems. A past that impinges, echoes, and whispers into the present of which it is part. Past as it may be, the past is only available to us in the present. This availability is not necessarily a ready one; these poems write of what persists: a persistence that acknowledges that our memories, and so to a great extent our selves, are dependent and reliant on place.

I returned to England, where I spent time as a boy, after seventeen years and kept finding places – canals, the painted doors and flower pots of narrow boats, the flint in an old wall – that brought back things I had forgotten. Sometimes these retrievals felt small, like a brush against your shoulder; other times the experience was more startling – rushes like fire up a flume, as memories seem to rush into the spaces between the present and the past. I'm tempted to say these experiences were a kind of reclamation, like finding a fallen stone from a ring in a field or remembering a word or name. Perhaps they were. But it felt more like the self plays host to passengers in us who will, on occasion, look through us like windows at the places to which they once belonged.

But of course the world is not only the site of our own memory. Each place is, I imagine, absolutely covered in the memories of others – such that a given place, if we could see those sites of contact, not entirely person and not entirely place, but a strange third, might appear like a pointillist painting, a sort of canvas of dots that comprise the personal whole. This, I feel, holds true no matter where we are, but seems easier to discern in some places and with some things than others.

Objects, paintings, and ruins invite the imagination to one of its favourite acts: to fill in gaps, to complete what was curtailed, to build, from a set of broken stairs, a staircase, into the air. They offer us an opportunity to make us aware that we are constantly in creative engagement with the world around us: fusions or marriages of self and other. Paintings, with which many of these poems are concerned, seem particularly capable of that invitation to see behind, to look under, to infuse a scene with the wider moment it suggests.

These poems, I hope, try to leave their own invitations to fill in or dream the self into. They are about the here and the gone, and the flooding of the latter into the former: the seawall between things through which pours memory, voices, and the traces of ourselves and others. They are then, also, I suppose, an attempt to embrace the feeling that there is a lessening in our engagement with the world as we give, with each glance or touch, some of the rations of our glances and touch to things; traces like the traces of those who were here before us, and who it's possible, on occasion, to hear singing, as it were, from the treeline.

*

THE INVENTION OF GLASS

Mercury in the belly of the lighthouse
walks light over the winter waves.
The landscape turns on its own slow greys.

This is the kettle lake where the wolf
stared down at the calf that fell through
the ice and froze. These are the pebbles

of its blue eyes turning from the right
to the left. Long after, and so long before
the invention of glass to cover our windows.

THE FISHERMAN

bent over a bucket, took out a knife
and turned the blade of it into the work,
scales fell silver, beryl, blue,
the smooth exactness of his hand flaring

in and out of his jacket – it wasn't just
me, but boys behind the streetlamps
and crates lashed with rope,
growing thin as their eyes went lucent,

light casting angles into the waves,
the knife in flashes coming as the bucket
brimmed with scales, blue, silver,
the boys almost nothings gone feral

in the shadows, a braille of eyes fixed
on the man conducting the bright
knife over the barrel and my body
thinning too as wings of brilliant silver

blue spread from the man's back who
flew away smiling over the waves.
I rushed in then with the other boys, all
wearing jackets that looked as if other men

had curled around them and fallen asleep,
rushed in on the bucket to try and eat
our fill of the scales, hungry for the bright
of them, the bright of our teeth turned

into the work as the streetlights brayed
peril over the breaking waves
and we did our jackets up men again:
ravenous and separate in our ways.

TUNNEL WALKING

1994
In a quarter-mile tunnel bored
through the heart of a hill, the lock keeper
lifted me high enough to feel the stone
our narrow boat slid under like an arm
through a sleeve. He said there used to be
men who would lay on their backs,
feet fit to the bricks in the ceiling,
pedalling dead freight through the dark.
How steam would replace them,

but not in time to save even one man
falling from the roofs of the boats
like meat from a bone. I stared down
into the water. Pale faces stared back up.

1999
The lock keeper sat in his basement
tracing his history back through the records
until the records gave way to a sound,
I imagined, like the cool exhalation of air
from the model train tunnels he'd cut
into the walls. He hummed a song
I recognised, but couldn't place, whenever
we drank from the mugs for brushes he used
to paint the miniature city behind his desk.
When he flicked them on with a little
white switch, I'd picture myself staring
back from one of the tiny windows.
I buried that sound when I was young,

2014
it pulses under the work I do
like the roar when you cover your ears
or the clouds above one of those men
laying in a bright field, practising the sky
forward as steam poured from his eyes
like the shallow barrels of a gun.
I think about him. About the last time
I saw the lock keeper: painting himself
deeper inside his miniature city, singing
in baritone as he fixed the moon to a wire.
About the sound, like a forest's heart after
a storm, of water dripping through moss
and loam. Of voyages we make alone.

A TIN OF ORANGES

So this is what it will be like
                    the impression in the sheets,

ingot on ingot of gold
                    blue air, *let there be at least*

a tin of oranges. I woke counting
                    back in decades and stood

behind the waterfall of
                    objects falling out of touch:

an ocean of shoes and loose
                    clothing, the antique bell on

the windowsill calling
                    the ancient children home

out of habit. Habit. The hands that reach
                    through the bedroom dark

part the air like curtains.
                    But I was already sailing

past my last day, the bed
                    a berth in the hull of a ship

on a sudden sea, my body folded
                    like the clothes across my knee.

ASHMOLEAN RINGS

People like clay less than painting.
The museum's pushed-back east wing
is not where the best windows are.
But the cabinets are crowded –
vases cluster behind their glass
like orphans waiting for a train.
A small flock of glances hovers
before the cordoned off display,
while crowds push inside the forests
painted in the adjacent room.
Dreams collected in this fork's tines:
what its owner (a bishop) craved,
the vows to himself he bandaged
carefully, each morning, the red
stains of beets on his wooden teeth –
unlike the painting where we can
always see the painter dimly
losing bet after bet to time.
We are given little glimpses,
can put them down to the sunlight,
the ring's shadow under a ring,
a ghost's finger jutting forward
and fifty years they wore the ring
erased whenever daylight drifts
through the window disfiguring
what the bishop heard after dusk.

Gold as honey but fat as slugs,
some rings look too big for fingers.
My watch with the glowing numbers,
how a child played with her toy horse

in the final evenings of Rome:
every time that we lose something
or some thing is lifted away
a shadow is left behind it.
Kids are fat with time as butter,
but old men are mostly shadows.
The pieces move across the board
like midnight crossing a table
where light perched to wash it feathers.
The sun sets, painters place their bets,
bishops swim from the tines of forks,
and the darkness rinses its tongue
in preparation for eating
today's heart out of tomorrow.

It's not a practical table.
It looks like a peacock's bright tail.
Each object a constellation,
each has a violin's bow held
against its face: you look to make
out what song the player will play.
Glint of silver, glint of a life,
it all goes under the hillside
until some little girl fishes
a garnet feather from the dirt.
In the red washes of the long
panel painting of a fox hunt,
ten riders ride into the dark,
except for one, who is riding
away from the trees with a hand
held up like a lantern shining.
The dark swallows. He lost his ring.
His love lies in another room

full of paintings, but he keeps on
lighting the impossible length
it would take to break from the paint.

At the centre of the forest
the fox pants in a hollow root.
The leaves shiver. Looking away,
distracted by all the sunlight,
the painter dashes between trees
and continues with his painting.
But staring into the canvas,
unable to do more than stare,
to run a finger over their lips
in the symbol of a lemon,
the painting makes itself a ghost
of the figure at its window.
Turning around, looking outside,
our own end remains hard to see –
just the birds pulling out the pins
that have pinned down the scenery.
The bishop sits mute with his fork.
The hunter holds his lamp so still
the paint around his hand is cracked.
That intruder shouldn't be here,
but he has come along with us:
however the curtains might part,
however the hunter might try
warming his hands by the firelight,
time drifted in the paint and froze.
A sun held just under the tongue,
a candle's glow against the teeth,
the painter smiles into the frame.
The hunter's lamp is lit with eyes.

It's only a mile to the Thames,
past the hard bones of the bishop,
who wouldn't, looking up, have known
fire meditated in his floor.
By the time it might get to us,
the smoke has already blown off
from the fires on the horizon.
What was, what is, but cannot stay:
the old song keeps alternating
like sound and silence on the page.
If it's lost then it is a world
and this one moves a bit quicker
than the string of newborn goslings,
and slower than the greying weir
losing its way under the oaks.
A young couple labours their boat
up the hillside with the canal,
as night gathers inside the locks.
What is left behind is as slight
as what shadows are left to sing
from lamps in the forest's heart
and the windows that blink open
in these old Ashmolean rings.

ST FRANCIS OF ASSISI

At this height, the rays of light grow
straighter, splitting cloud

cover, making mountains lighter
in their burden. Francis spreads

his wings, a faint V ferrying up
the dead and leaving each

accumulated sorrow to fall back
in rain like salt fermenting mist.

For the living, who sleep in the mist.
Red Wolf, Black Rhino, the Dusky

Sparrow. Too heavy? Too many.
Francis, who won't stop working,

works with the broken neck of a swan.
Something must be wrong.

THE COLD KILN

Bent white paper. I smooth it out.
Could be the tired face of a moon.
Or a night by the cove. Alone,
the trees' courage that, yes, the briar

of the silent world might compass us
into what sustains the long-masted
forests sailing in their place, or some
flare at the back of the tongue

warm our words under what the cold
kiln of coastal light splays on the sand.
On the sleeping whale of a boulder,

uncurl a hand from around our flash-
light and see across the wave-backs if
an answer to divide the aloneness comes.

AFTERWARDS

The streets were very quiet. Traffic thinned.
People walked less and less outside the windows.
Trees knew nothing, it was spring, and each
bud unravelled its pale green-yellow hands.
The sunlight sat in their hands.

That ice-cream truck I'd learned to hate,
ringing its bells even when it was raining,
rang its bells. And then they didn't ring.
There was almost nothing on the shelves.
We moved the bed into the living room,

and the living room into the bedroom
so that you could close the door and work.
My friend from Milan grew thick and sad.
Months, he said, before he would see his parents.
He played the drums on a pillow with a spoon.

You told me just before it began to happen
that you hadn't been happy here for months.
There was nowhere to go. People walked by
less and less. You opened and closed the door.
I stood by the door, my hands unravelling.

TO PRONOUNCE THE MAN

Sometimes I think I hear a key scratch,
but that's probably just Susan
under the floor like a seismograph
waiting to come up the stairs in her
fuchsia robe yelling about *the noise*.

He never leaves and I never see him.
When I moved in the landlady catalogued
the virtues behind each door.
Her quick glance at his window
has been slow to pronounce the man.

I've come to the door once to find
the police telling me I can *go back inside*.
I hadn't come outside or seen the line
so clearly drawn between what they do
and what needs doing. At five

the light here is nothing. A thawing blue.
I saw him then, wading into the sun
like a wave of glue. He, who even then,
must be father and daughter to himself.
Mother, and brother, and son.

SPIDER

When it is night you are there
in the spaces between wood slats

under the roofs where you spin
a harness of silk waiting on

the fibres of the sky as the lamp
light cycles further in the darkness

not even the moon can find you –

STONES AND SWEEPER

What news do you bring us?
   It's October. The leaves have fallen.

From where? The thicket on the slope?
   No. Higher on the ridges, the oaks.

What of the ranger? Of the coast?
   The tine of his lantern on the coast.

Who will sweep the leaves from our stones?
   I will sweep the leaves from the stones.

Like the woman painted the watches' hands?
   Yes, pointing the brushes with their tongues.

You will come to us? October and October?
   October and October and October.

And in the meantime? Where will you go?
I will be with the ranger.

Upon the coast?
The thin tine of his lantern on the coast.

We will wait by our stones.
My radium ghosts in the radium oaks.

*

CHAD CAMPBELL's first collection, *Laws & Locks* (Signal Editions, 2015) was nominated for the Gerald Lampert Memorial Award for Best Debut Collection. His poems have appeared or are forthcoming in: *The Walrus*, *Best Canadian Poetry 2015*, *The New Wave: An Anthology of Canadian Poetry*, *Poetry Ireland Review*, *The Scores*, and *Arc*, among others. He is studying for a PhD at the University of Manchester's Centre for New Writing, where he co-edits *The Manchester Review*. His second collection is due out in Canada in 2021.

Speaking with a few poet friends we're all at similar stages now, counting poems, whispering in the small hours, asking: *Do I have a book? Might I actually have a book? Surely I don't have a book?* It's exciting and terrifying: thinking, for the first time, of book as medium, book as form. How the poems might speak across pages. How one might use repetition, sequence etc. I definitely didn't set out to write a book. It's always been poem by poem for me. I think the second I decide to write a book will be the second I never write a poem again. Or the book I end up writing will resemble some kind of dreadful concept album. I tend to just write about whatever I'm preoccupied with.

In my mind the poems featured here are adolescent – emo poems if you will. Long hair ripped jeans lip ring cigarette behind the bike sheds poems. But not in any self-deprecating way. I don't use adolescent as a qualifier for childish or unfinished. I say adolescent because the poems, like me, are still very much obsessed with childhood trauma; they are, for want of a better phrase, trying to make sense of childhood. I think it was Chen Chen who said: 'my poems are braver than I am' and this applies perfectly to me. The poems featured here are me at my bravest. Because they are me at my most vulnerable.

Mental illness, alcoholism, domestic violence run in my family. As a kid they were my reality. They are my reality. And for this reason I'm particularly interested in the violences we inherit. Habitualised, generational violences, be they big or small, be they directed at oneself or a loved one, and to what extent our lives are predetermined. Can we write a different story? I could reel off a list: working class masculinity, loss, fatherhood, Guinness, grizzly bear, field, shotgun... but I'd rather not. I think these poems are me asking the future if everything will be OK. I think these poems are me asking the future for forgiveness.

*

THE MINOTAUR

Six Lies

The Minotaur tells his sixth lie of the day
to a colleague, seventh to the bus driver,
eighth to himself as he pays for a Twix,
smiling down at the woman behind the till.

His ninth he tells to a pooing dog,
tenth to its shadow, eleventh to its walker
who nods gravely, opening a pink plastic bag.
The Minotaur finds a bench by a fountain

and there he unwraps the Twix, promising
as he peels away the shiny paper
that he won't eat chocolate again for a month.
A man in a suit and six o'clock stubble is asking

where the nearest train bridge is and *are they frequent?*
In the corner of the room the radio speaks words
like rips of Velcro. The Minotaur pads the landing,
golden wrapper rustling in his pocket like a bird.

All the Devil's Mess

Because this is any other Saturday
the Minotaur is walking his invisible dog
in the park, clumping through snow
towards the iced brown pond

where the quilted backs of silver-
haired men huddle at the jetty,
whizzing their remote-controlled
boats across its island of melt water.

Because this is any other Saturday
the Minotaur is unsheathing
a tennis racket and ball. He's winking
at the men, his eyelashes lined with snow.

This evening, in a pub's dark corner,
hear them whisper of horns, of a bark and a ball
and boats lost and ice snapped like chipboard,
of a pond folded once, like a table.

The Moon

The Minotaur is convinced he has swallowed the moon.
He googles *irrational fear of moon swallowing*
and walks the park at night looking up at the moon,
touching the spot where he knows

the real moon is lodged. A baby on the tube
pokes the moon in his throat
and the Minotaur's flinch short-circuits
the carriage lights, makes the baby cry.

The Minotaur tells this story to Dr Reynolds,
swallowing it deeper and deeper with every word.
Have you ever tried throwing up the moon?
On his 40th birthday the Minotaur lifts the moon

from its place above the dusty paperbacks.
He pockets it, takes it swimming
the following day with his six-year-old daughter,
forgets the moon in a café one afternoon, tells no one.

AND GOD SAID

Every time a horse lies down in a sunlit field
an island goes up off the coast of Alaska or Peru
or in the middle of a lake south of Stockholm.
Every time a whale is born albino
a man doesn't die of liver failure and every time
it rains at sea a child speaks first words.
Every time you watch the football
in your alcoholic father's flat
on his little settee that unfolds into a bed
in case you ever wanted to stay
a forest disappears and a doorbell rings.
Every time the ref blows the whistle
and your father boils the kettle and somewhere
islands are going up and oil rigs just watching.

DEAR POSTIE

If no answer please leave parcel behind rhododendron –
if storm hits and rhododendron blows away
please leave parcel inside wheelie bin with brick on top –
if crying baby can be heard on approach
tap three times on bottom-left panel of shed window –
DO NOT ring doorbell – if rainbow windmill
spins slower than usual open phone and call alcoholic father –
if rainbow windmill stops spinning at any moment
come back in month with picture of alcoholic father
eating fish and chips in park – if phone rings out
wait for nesting swallows to return from Africa
then call again – DO NOT mention alcoholic father
to friends colleagues woman you love – DO NOT
kiss woman you love – DO NOT eat sleep
shit watch TV until alcoholic father is spotted
leaving Tesco with Guinness and Hula Hoops –
DO NOT I repeat DO NOT drive to 24-hour Shell garage
spend following afternoon outside alcoholic father's flat
old ladies watching – bay windows blue with Countdown.

THE CHILDREN

on the muted screen a ball lands
one side of a line
and this means that a person has won
the camera jiggles
zooms out refocuses on a crowd
who are cheering
which means that a person has won
yes clapping
back smacking drink dropping
all signifiers
that yep a ball has landed
one side of a line
one side not one side but ONE
SIDE of course right
because a person has won
a ball has landed
people are happy and although this is not
a metaphor for grief
I cannot deny that a ball not a ball but
THE BALL
has landed is landing will land
until it stops being
THE BALL and starts being a ball
at the edge of
a roofless room lots of people are
jumping around in-
side of lots of sound lots of screens
lots of open sky and
did I mention my dad has taken a
shotgun to a field
and I haven't realised because I am
watching tennis

which means my dad has decided
is deciding
will decide to become not a dad
but THE DAD
is asking a man for a shotgun is
saying can I buy
yes bring me this much and it's a
man from the pub
someone I'll walk past for years
which means I am
existing in relation to this moment
my sister is
eating a choc ice romping around
the garden holding
a toad in relation to this pocket of
time my mum
zipping up our puffer jackets pulling
down our hats
while my dad walks through rain
to an ATM
leaves a room with a shotgun in a
duffle bag
this moment almost encased in
glass
this skyscraper I am not really watching
tennis inside of
not on my lunch break not
twenty six
but nine years old being pulled out of
maths
my sister four whole years
barely taller

than a table and we are not children
anymore
but THE CHILDREN THOSE CHILDREN
THAT CHILD

THE FATHER HEAVENS

After Buddhism at the British Library, 25 October 2019 – 29 February 2020

Father Cosmology

This cosmological map depicts the heavenly
realm called 82a Wytham Street with palaces, gardens
and marketplaces for the 33 fathers who reside there.
In the middle is the settee of the father
Daniel who is lord of this heaven. See
the hot rock hole, the ancient shape of a backside.
Take a seat. Oh, you've done that before. This is one
of six heavens or celestial realms.

Fathers of Previous World Cycles

In the Theravāda tradition, four fathers are believed
to have attained Nirvana. The history of these fathers
is given in a text which is traditionally read
to sons in the bath. Kukusandha father
(top) is the first father, Koṇāgamana is the second
father, Kassapa is the third father and the
historical father Daniel born as Our Prince Danny
is the fourth and final father of this era. Every
father has always achieved enlightenment
in the shadow of a certain tree.

Great Peacock Wisdom King

This manual contains paintings of altars for
sons who will one day become fathers
and may end up alone in a flat or may not.
One father can be seen riding a peacock, a bird that
keeps a territory free from snakes. Can you spot
the note left three years ago saying *I've hoovered?*
Yes, a faint smell of skin and Hula Hoops. On the right
a father appears in a stylised wheel. Between
the spokes are the names for certain kinds of shadow.

Life Father

Fatherhood is described as a series of manifestations
that are impermanent. It is thought that there
is no ultimate reality in things – every father
is subject to change and to some extent
dependent (dep / en / dent) on perception.
Sonhood does not encourage
belief in a creator deity or
supreme being. However, where
have you walked to this Sunday morning?
Get up from this settee. Close that empty fridge.
See the years of letters at the door?
Gather them up.

54 QUESTIONS FOR THE MAN WHO SOLD A SHOTGUN TO MY FATHER

Is tea an exact science / Are willow trees categorically sad / Can a house have a face / Are astronauts real / How many bad things have been witnessed by just deer / Is hiking peaceful / Are skyscrapers pretty / Was there an imposter at the wake / What does flamingo taste like / Are bees kind / Is the BBC right / Do lemmings understand / Are children who lose a parent to suicide more likely to die the same way / How many kettles are whistling right now / How many tractors will break down today / What did the first nectarine smell of / Where are all the dead ducks / Do whales dream / How many Boeing 737s have successfully landed since 2002 / How old is the oldest tree in Alaska / Which shade of orange was your son's bedroom this morning / How many rivers are there between my body and yours / Is stilton your favourite cheese / Have you ever been to Budapest / Do you have an opinion on Coldplay / Do you remember your ninth birthday / Do you fly well / Do you burp more often than you think you should / Are you hairy / How many mugs have you dropped / Have you ever stroked an elephant / At what age did you stop believing in Santa / How many weddings have you attended / Do you enjoy French films / Have you ever been operated on / Is your garden south-west facing / Do you own a pair of secateurs / Would you call yourself a family man / Were you ever any good at tennis / Is your penis longer than mine / Does it rain in your weather / Is there a bus / Are you waiting by the frozen fruit in Aldi / Wearing a beanie / Listening to Eminem / Did he tell you what he wanted it for / Did you ask / Did he smile / Did you touch / Talk much / Had he shaved / If you could use a number to describe his laugh would you use 1000 or 3 / Did you put the money towards a loft extension / Is that a lasagne in your oven?

MY FATHER IS SITTING ON THE OTHER SIDE OF THE FRENCH DOORS

just sitting, like a grizzly bear I shoo away in June.
Back hunched, staring at the ground, a red biro
tucked behind his ear. I like to think
he's marvelling at the patio we dug,
the pebble path I skipped school to help lay,
or planning for another pond, another
row of sunflowers by the wall.
                                        Right on cue
the cat arrives and figure-of-eights a plant pot
as my father itches the back of her neck with the biro,
flicks greenflies from his shirt.
I can never wake early from this dream,
never sprint fast enough down the landing, never
unzip the blinds, swing open the window in time to hear
the thud of his footsteps over the shed roof,
branches bouncing back to stillness.
And I'll never know – how could I? –
that in this dream he'd grow old, grow fur, eventually.
The locals think I'm crazy –
they say you shouldn't feed the bears – *dumb Brit*.
They say a grizzly will return for a lifetime to the spot
it once found food, the exact kink of river,
stubby bush, overflowing garbage can;
but I do it anyway, always at night, barefoot, just in case
he comes, my father, sniffs me out,
calls off this silly game, crosses the Atlantic, Canada –
and I'm already gone –
he'll see my shoes tucked behind the glass,
laces still in a bow,

and he'll think no different; he'll wait, he'll sit,
back hunched, staring at the ground,
till August ends and the bears, wide-eyed,
come for him too.

IMPACTS

It happens next summer when the car in front turns left
at the motel sign and a doe notices just in time
to blink and a man with a bag of beers looks
but doesn't slow any.
Or tonight, when I wake
to your naked arm cold and too heavy
so my breath holds as I pretend not to feel, pretend
I didn't catch its eye and, for a second
consider braking left
on a year I'm yet to live. It happens
on a bridge over a train track, a father back for a weekend, a son
propped on the railings
arms in a V, altogether unaware of the light's red to amber,
the freight around the bend, its horn
an impact that will whoosh through him, keep him
quiet all the way home
up there on his father's shoulders.

PANASONIC RF-P50DEG-S

they
must
have
known
more
than
they
let
on
the
birds
you
would
probably
laugh
both
hands
deep
in
your
pockets
and
looking
up
as
you
do
because
hey
I've
got
this

radio
I
can't
give
you
and
there's
a
wheel-
barrow
in
my
garden
full
to
bursting
with
feathers
I
didn't
ask
for

IN AMBER

In my dream you are almost drunk,
struggling with the lock on the french doors
of my childhood, a lit cigarette
cupped in your palm.

Seconds before I wake, I realise
I've no idea which side you're on, which side
of those huge lime-scaled sheets of glass
you huddle to, hunched and cursing

the key which catches as you turn it. Sure,
the garden lurks behind, the gravel path,
but so does the television, the empty fish tank,
the cat's water bowl. So, which side are you on,

and where does that leave me?
Give me a clue – nod, blink, catch my eye,
crunch a snail shell, ash your cigarette,
flick the butt so I might hear it land.

If I could reach I'd pluck a silver hair from your arm,
just one, like a dream's very own pinch,
a dream we'll both wake from, at the same time,
on the sofa, some film playing ... *Did you feel it too?*

from BLOCK SEQUENCE

v. Draw a circle around the city you grew up in

look / the field you lost your virginity in / isn't far from the field your dad stopped breathing in / isn't far from the field he taught you how to ride a bike in / isn't far from the field normal families (which included yours for a while) used to picnic in / isn't far from the field he coached your football team in / isn't far from the field he watched you play cricket in / isn't far from the field you smoked your first cigarette in / isn't far from the field your ninth birthday went well then went wrong in / your tenth birthday went well then went well then went wrong in / your twelfth birthday went wrong in / isn't far from the field other families went quiet in / isn't far from the field a few birds lifted from the trees in / isn't far from the field your mum refused to remove her sunglasses in / the restaurant / parents evening / even at breakfast in her dressing down her coffee smoking her lip only slightly puffy

vi. Epigraph

rain / school play / next week / Scheherazade / beggar / face paint / field at the edge of / dog's name / letter P / maths / sitting next to / Lucy Hollingsworth / Helly Hansen / field at the edge of / come outside / corridor / against this wall / book bags / coats / dog's name / Abingdon Road / past Londis / field at the edge of / Mrs Burton / offers you / a custard cream / a special chair / your sister is / waiting / your sister / field at the edge of / maths / school play / six miles / rain / Helly Hansen with the / yellow toggles / Lucy Hollingsworth / brown hair / empty chair / fractions / book bags / face paint / school nurse / field at the edge of / sister / behind a window / past a PE lesson / Matt Fricker shouts / skipping rope / Londis / school play / next week / willow trees / fractions / beggar / face paint / field at the edge of / come outside / Mrs Burton / biscuit / dog's name / for once / not frowning / but also / not / not frowning / your sister is / rain / six miles / field at the edge of / say it / field at the edge of / goddammit / say it / Mum's on the way / just fucking / say it / brown hair / empty chair / against this wall / say it / field at the edge of / willow trees / field at the edge of / deep breathes / field at the edge of / sister is / saying / but he was / snoring / this morning / field at the edge of Kennington field at the edge of Kennington field at the edge of Kennington field at the edge of Kennington field at the edge of Kennington field at the edge of Kennington field at the edge of Kennington field at the edge of Kennington field at the edge of Kennington field at the edge of Kennington field at the edge of Kennington

*

JOE CARRICK-VARTY is a British-born Irish writer and co-founder of *bath magg*. He is the author of two pamphlets: *Somewhere Far* (The Poetry Business, 2019), which won the 2018 New Poets Prize, and *54 Questions for the Man Who Sold a Shotgun to My Father* (Out-Spoken Press, 2020). His poems have appeared in the *New Statesman*, *Poetry Review* and *Poetry Ireland Review*. He lives in London.

These are poems from a settled life. From such a position you can look at the world calmly and thoughtfully. In my poems peace seems often to be a theme, sometimes simply with reference to the absence of war, as in 'Milk', sometimes as a state of daily life. Often language bursts through, in a seizing of things by their names or in the joyful feeling of creative possibilities, as in 'Walking through Slack', the village near the top of the drive at Arvon's Lumb Bank centre. Being a Christian also underlies my view of life, bringing an understanding of the need for hope, though this isn't always easy to achieve - as in 'Stained Glass.' Having been happily married for a long time, however, is a constant help. After marriage, we lived first in a university flat, then for nearly fifty years in the same house with a big garden, before finally moving to a second floor flat with extensive views. This did not, as I had feared, cause the poems to dry up but rather generated more, beginning with 'Moving Day'.

Growing up in the fortunate generation of free Direct Grant schools and free university tuition, I was introduced to a generous breadth of literature. Decades later in retirement I filled in some of the long gap since graduating by doing an M.A. in Contemporary Poetry at Sheffield University, including a dissertation on Seamus Heaney. Nothing stays contemporary, but one can keep reading.

The first contemporary poet who sparked my sense of new powers of writing was Thom Gunn, whose second collection *The Sense of Movement* I borrowed from the library in about 1959. I was entranced by the poem 'The Nature of an Action' with its magical last lines 'Much like the first, this room in which I went. / Only my being there is different.' Many years later, one of the poets who has resonated with me most clearly has been Heaney, who I heard read at Attingham Park when he was touring his newly published first volume *Death of a Naturalist*. Of all his collections, *Seeing Things* is the one I value above all. A later discovery was Eavan Boland, with poems about the intrusion of another layer of existence into ordinary life as in 'The War Horse' and again in a different sense, 'The Achill Woman' where the writer's realisation of her own blinkered perception of life beyond literature expressed something of myself. Following her sudden death, we await the publication of her, alas posthumous, collection *The Historians* in the autumn.

Occasionally of course something in particular may generate a poem. 'Were there Trams in Odessa?' grew quite suddenly from a question which I just caught without its context one morning on Radio 3. Later I learnt that the presenter had been referring to David Oistrakh and his place of birth and to the trams of Manchester, but by then I was deep into an image of a to me unknown city at the turn of the twentieth century and the realisation that my knowing nothing about it fed, rather than obstructing, this image – how the mind 'mixes memory and invention.' I wrote to the presenter, Petroc Trelawny, and it became Radio 3's 'Friday Poem' one week, with a credit to *PN Review*.

*

WALKING THROUGH SLACK

The village street tips me out into hills.
I watch the clouds canter on slopes far off,
on crests of the grassy mountains.
The midday peace is warm and edible.

Slackening pace at the lane's top, I see
the circle of the world.
Wonderful, the great presences of land
the sun is making play with

and wonderful in the mind how thoughts that lay
like stones in a dark landscape
moving at last
prepare themselves for speech.

MILK

War's end:
we were resuming, in a shadowy world,
the burden of peace;
patiently, patiently beginning.
Outside the infants' dining hall
two air-raid shelter humps
(haunted, they said)
resembled graves.

Milk, white among dampness,
waited for playtime.
Job's Dairy, the bottle told me:
a patriarch, unseen in early morning,

clattering to school with rough crates
tangling his windy beard.

Then a first ha'porth of learning took hold of me:
it was job, like a job,
like something simple you get up and do.
War finished, you begin on peace
like a favourite pudding.

Later I was told, no, it was Jōb.
Peace harsh on the tongue,
chewy and difficult,
was cold and necessary like milk.
Single planes overhead at night
droned like speeches; through lanes at evening
went canvassers foraging for votes.

Milk, day by day appearing,
washed into us by ounces knowledge
of the new world and its ways.
At our next school
quiet men from big new dairies
made the deliveries, anxious about their rent.

POINT OF BALANCE

I'm standing in the hall.
To my left, a commentator is amazed
about a long putt birdied at the twelfth.
Someone is coming down the stairs, declaring
United are ahead; behind me
a plaintive voice asks why this lampshade wobbles.

I'm trying to discuss when tea should happen.
The cat sulks past, upset by a strange toy
bought to amuse him. I get vague replies.
The phone rings; urgent feet thump to an answer.
My aged washing machine rocks into spin;
the TV peppers no one with applause.

The lampshade voice is gauging shades of blue;
the cat, consoled, slicks down his marmalade;
September yellows softly in; our world
must turn some more before the dark.
My focus switches, balancing, attention
pulled thinly sideways as the moments pass.

NAMING THE WEEDS

Sunday. I walk the garden path
where sun-blotched paving warms my feet.
This border's rich confusion shows me
weeds whose generations
are fifty years, a hundred years
older than the house, the street.
I name their blossoming:
            violet, figwort, viper's bugloss, vetch.

Our garden logs the years
in layers of planted hopes, yet weeds endure,
old words tucked under the hem of speech,
leafing up unnoticed till a sudden colour
lights the hedge bottom and reminds me,
sends me back to the flower book to be sure

I'm naming them right:
        enchanter's nightshade, self-heal, fox-and-cubs.

A rain shower drives me in, to move aside
leaf patterned curtains and stare out
across a garden full of words. Tansy, *etym. unknown,*
perhaps linked to the Greek for immortality,
holds up its yellow buttons. I watch seasons pass
while buried names like little bursts of thought
spring from neglected corners:
        coltsfoot, bittercress, toadflax, poppy, spurge.

SARDINIA

Moored Boats

That man and wife who kiss
out in the sea between the moored boats
are German, it appears.
Her black, Babylonian cap
describes her as a thriving dress-shop owner.
They swim about together.
Walking on sand, he shows a heavy figure:
she smiles at him, fair-haired on land,
and buoys him up.

Afternoon Wind

The wind of afternoon shivers the trees.
Think of it as a brown goat,
hot, small, distant,
picking its way over dry country.

Think of it as a fish,
slipping through clearness, crossing water
in swift glides.
Think of it in winter as a coach
rocking through mountains, black with rain.

SIGNAL

Before the days of texting, here's my mother
leaning across the sink to tap the window
at my father, weeding.
She places one index finger across the other: 'Tea.'
Looking up, he waves,
turns to survey his work then parks the hoe.
She fills the pot, carries the tray through.

The nestling's gape, the ladybird's spotted badge
give meaning without words: the tulip offers
its stripey bugle; yellow flowers
primp the forsythia. Under the little bridge
small dappled fish declare themselves as gravel.
The lonely man hang-gliding over Stanage Edge
feels what the winds tell as they clear the ridge.

Now after so long, you and I
find ourselves humming tunes the other started
in a different room, or guessing thoughts
from a slight inflection, look or trick of the eye.
Invited to 'tweetle' when tea's ready, I 'Olly, olly!'
the old Cam racers' cry, to call my cox,
deep in twelfth-century rivalry, from his books.

STAINED GLASS

Unchanged for centuries. Yet the saint's feet
darken as her halo thins, her motto pales.
Glass creeps, liquid, down into her toes.
She is becoming earthly again.

Her cloak still throws blood on the stone floor.
Could heaven abandon her after all this time?
She stares out as though ready to suffer her martyrdom anew.
Meanwhile she is claimed like us by gravity

which insists on weightiness.
Though defiant, her stance admits
that she is always sinking,
and sanctity is heavy work and never finished.

DEPARTURE

Sitting in the top-floor study
I look out at clouds and think
I could open this window and step through.
I kneel on the desk, free the latch and clamber
into the sky, one hand on the tiles to steady me.
The breeze that suddenly pulls me free is warm.

Now I am cycling the air, legs and arms
working as though in water as I find my way
bit by bit over the tall trees opposite.
Seeing the floodlights of United's ground
I set a course, buffeted by soft gusts,
and meet a crowd of airborne travellers.

Nice day! a woman calls as we sweep down
and settle on the station roof like pigeons.
Daddy, why are we here? a child asks.
He tells her quietly, *This is the terminus.*
Now all at once I see – we are the dead
waiting in this warm spot for heaven to open.

A stir begins. We start to look about
and see below on Platform One somebody
holding a whistle. *Here we go! At last!*
the cry goes up. *Look there!* The clouds are parting
clear over Sheffield station and a tall angel
in boots and golden tunic waves us through.

WERE THERE TRAMS IN ODESSA?

(overheard question)

Sepia. Tall house-fronts, pale above the dark streets.
Three tiny figures in heavy coats,
walking. What year is it?

It is the sepia year of long ago.
There was no time then. Streets were empty,
shops unvisited.

Inscrutable stillness, the camera's moment
fixed against the flickering human eye.
Caged in history.

No. The picture's imagined, conjured up
by that creative tool the hopeful brain
which mixes memory and invention.

But such a place and such a year existed
outside the mind's embroidery. There was trade,
there were marriages,

as in the nameless photographs which drop
out of an album from your mother's youth –

But then of course they knew if there were trams.
An easy question.

THE COWS

In the middle of the night the cows came
breathing their hay-breath into the silent kitchen
and I, turning in my cold bed above,

was also there among them - felt their motherly warmth,
saw their shadowed flanks, gleam of damp muzzles,
sensed the flick of their tails across the cupboards.

Companionable silence. So I slept,
woke with the light, looked out and saw the herd
leaving in a slow walk over the meadow.

HIDE

A wooden silence so dark
the floor is invisible, the shutters
defined only by blades of sunlight.
We feel our way to a bench,
steadying our feet between its uprights,
settle, pause.

When we open up
it's the fourth day of creation.
Moorhen and coot, grebe ferrying their young,
pattern the lake's glitter with black and brown
while over the teeming water mallard fly.
Dazzled, we stare

as though we had entered
a world beyond our knowledge
and come upon a different use for seeing
or as though sight itself invented
this fine embroidery of clouds and ripples,
of birds and air.

MOVING DAY

One, two, three

   and we vault

      across the valley and land

here in another postcode
where a squirrel fossicks in the rain
on the moss-lumpy roof of now our garage
and the back of my mind says
when we get home
but we are home.

We wake to a mild, damp day
and walls of boxes. Oddments which can't be returned
to drawers which are ours no longer.
The unencumbered squirrel sits on its haunches
and enjoys the air.

We are in the sky,
living among treetops in the region
fir cones drop from. Out of the window
we sense the passing traffic of radio waves.

The future crouching in the valley
opens its arms as the sun rises and the row of pines
retract their shadows and whisper of possibilities.
We empty and stow, fight through our box walls like prisoners
digging a way out. Evening comes.

Morning comes, the fourth day. Birds look in at us
from their neighbourly branches. We are here
for keeps. Day passes. Far down the valley
an owl couches his soft notes on silence.

*

JENNY KING was born in London during the Blitz. Her
parents, both teachers of German, encouraged her in writing
poetry as a child and struggled with wartime paper rationing
to make her a book to write them in. She studied English
at Cambridge, taught for three years in Shrewsbury, then
married and moved to Sheffield, where she and her husband,
a medieval historian, have lived ever since. She has continued
to write, with poems in a wide variety of magazines including
PN Review, The North, Stand, The Rialto, Orbis and a number
of others now sadly extinct, such as *Smiths Knoll, Staple,
Iron* and *Outposts*, as well as several yearly PEN anthologies.
In 2003 a poem of hers came second in the Bridport Prize
competition. The first of her three pamphlets, *Letting the Dark
Through*, (Mandeville Press 1981) had its roots in an Arvon
course with Peter Scupham and George Szirtes; the other
two, *Tenants* (2014) and *Midsummer* (2020), are published
by Smith|Doorstop and owe a great deal to Ann and Peter
Sansom's Poetry Business workshops and support.

A few years ago, a leading Danish poet said in an interview that if a poem or novel did not concern itself with the current global crisis of our climate, he was not interested in reading it.

However sympathetic to that particular cause one may indeed be, an artistic environment so limited in scope must necessarily be stifling to writers and readers alike. The political work of art, as it is now conceived, has become unbearably concrete. The work must deal directly with global warming or else fail to qualify even as legible material. And yet, reading the works of, say, Percy Bysshe Shelley today, there can be no doubt about their artistic and political relevance, and yet Shelley fails to mention green house gases even once.

The issue is decidedly *not* whether one should create unpolitical works (whatever that might mean). The issue, rather, is that our understanding of what is potentially political has shrunk. John Ashbery has said that all great art was to him political, in the sense that it makes one want to improve in every aspect of life. The implication is not only that everything is in some way political (a familiar truism), but equally that our politics are an expression of how we perceive ourselves and the world around us, and that an awareness of ourselves inevitably leads to an awareness of others. The implication also – one that is not as absurd as it may at first seem – is that a poem about birds or hills or flowers has at least the potential to make us behave differently as political animals.

The illusion that some works are political and some are not is closely bound to another equally illusory idea; the notion that, because political art must be allied with progress, art itself must also 'progress'. But art does no such thing. It is pointless to say that the plays of Aeschylus are less evolved or refined than the novels of Henry James, say, or the poems of Inger Christensen. This is important not just because one should be able to read without the numbing preconceptions of historicism, but because any appreciation of our current political urgency must recognise that we are defined by the past we imitate as much as by the past we want to break away from. In others words, to censure Aeschylus or James or Christensen for not dealing with our present reality is to miss what they have offered us, and still do, here and now.

Novels and poems must be allowed to speak in every way, to examine every thing, to present every problem. This goes equally for the issues of the past, social or otherwise, as for the soft apartheid still deeply entrenched in the politics of the United States, to choose one relevant example. It goes equally for the social issues of the 19th century as for the climate we may or indeed may not leave behind after the 21st. If our literature is not capable of representing whatever it wants, to present whichever problem it deems worthy of attention, then we have lost something very valuable: our ability to think without constraints, to write plays or novels or poems without limit.

*

DETACHED RETINA

Love is the thing. It walks over late at night
To breathe in the fine blues of his wardrobe,

To watch, as if over the stirring of tea, the shaking
Drifts of white, the steam lifting itself across

His pinkish belly, his seemingly useless locales –
Armpit, say. He sees small bodies of pine,

Pink limbs needled against a rimless sky –
A flash to whiten his squiggly reds. No idea

What shifts beneath the pattern of what is, what
Paints birds' feathers, what lights the morning,

In his streaming kimono, flashes over stone.
Half-blind, he waits for changes in the gray

Edges of his thought, a bronze light submerged.
Some clarity is known to him: how one weaves.

OF WHERE TO BEGIN

A man offers you a dry red wine
directly from the bottle. You can
smell the knowledge on him.

You tend not to show your best
impressions to strangers. They may
prefer the fraudulent if

illustrious wave, the image as
surface, this glass stained yellow
to be passed and reflected

in sickly overcast. Knowing
the kind of food they serve here,
you turn down the brownish olive,

the crude rhubarb pie, that thing
you were certain held cilantro.
Then he comes back,

the waiter, leaving his tip
for you to divine. It occurs then
that the eye catches itself

in the very act of seeing.
You realise the ocean is
any number of reflections.

HOLIDAY WITH THE KNUDSENS

The finch is far out now,
though it is too late to assume
any normalcy of things as
some predetermined distance.
The finch never leaves
much behind – though it returns
for whatever it was. I was
once here as well, present
for the return of finches, all
yellow-breasted yolks

impossibly alive between
this coldly lit summer house
and some purplish distance.

PALM TREES

These beaches here: they sang
Last night your praises.
They broke among the waves,
Blathered away with each fall

And rise of their blue thought.
Between their lines, your face
Billowed like a sail –
Between their winds, the word

Spoke something about God,
About His wandering here, also,
To sleep long nights through the cold.
These flashes of sand are His,

If you believe in that sort of thing,
And even the forlorn view of sandals
Spooling on the water's edge.
Yet you are known only to yourself

As someone frail and angry; you
Recall slow shapes of palm trees
Turning greens to new golds;
You recall yourself in their shade.

THE YEAR OF SONG

He is away beneath the bridge
because the cops can't get to him
and neither can you. Stark, freezing
blade – his flaked collar shattered
to its core – he holds one shoulder
as though letting go would split
the bone once more. This crazy
town we're having, drowning
the noise of life ebbing from
his bluelit corpse. Yet, getting up
(and this is where your story begins),
the man bares you his nakedness.
He wears nothing but the soul
of the boy whose life he took,
t shirt in relentless dark, purple
reds like clouds rekindling lakes:
Old Joe, truckstop gasoline
peddler who wore his faith across
the chest, who let down a window
and called, Get outta there you
crazed kid you'll freeze to death.
A cut moon slips his gold
light past and shows
his skin lit through, a yellow
like old paper, like the sun.
Soon the man refires, his nerve
back to life. Go to hell, he says.
He snaps his fingers like snow
flung to jump and pivot in the air,
his toes a wild elderberry, blackened
to the vein. (You did not see
the abandoned lots of dandelion,

the rows of cars turning eastward
through barely lit evenings.)
He stumbles, gets up to lean
on the world. Go to hell, he says.
But he'll never drop, you think, we
all will die before he gets that cold.

IN ON IT

A day like any other:
The fine tuning of the weather,
The wooded sections withering on –
The quiet reaches of the surf
Stranger and stranger in the reeds.

The new slip of the sound
Closing its mind about us. Unfathomable
Reaches of the air, dithering
Lives of small birds through blue.
How the cold touches this wild room –

How the hail of the grand piano
Sounds this winter's small approach.
How the music of a lessened thing,
These blue chords rattling along,
Leaves us scattered and weightless.

The day is one of restlessness,
Of light sleep and few arrangements.
We reach for the slipshod wave,
The waters touching water –
The old news of some abandoned beach.

SOME WEATHER

And so the rain
sleeted the curious heirloom.
The wind stooped the trees from
their winding ascents, yellowed
their bodies with language.
There is being after this
mottled persistence
within each crag top and shaggy bustling
heather in the reeds; there is
the jostling of silt, lichen,
the dried stalks that darkness falls
suddenly upon. There is the rain
returning to us its findings –
this rain that seeks us here where
one thing must follow the other,
parades glowing underneath a staggering of waves,
this slanted brick and stone
flawed in their light. There is
this rain that clouds these cities
in sequences of ash heaps and scraggy lows:
it will slip into the order of things
as they appear to be, as thoughts
scattered over dirt roads.

MARBLE

Dimly the stone
recalls a spangled sea –

wave on wave of
blue-lit chimes in

this rocky light. One
addresses this blue,

as you are wont to do
crossing your blue bridge

on mildly strange after-
noons. Being yourself

remnant in nature,
you ebb also

with coral reefs and shells
falling and rising yet

falling. You speak of the sea
as if it would return

one day to stay your bridge
along the edges – shape

the land blue and pale
with blue. But the sea

does not spin or pivot
or roll: it remains

in blue repose, no more
than the fragment of a thing,

bare and small and partial.

THINGS AS THEY MUST BE

Then on the way we left behind
the apples and their blossoms, the system
threatening to change most things into
something else. The assembly of fruit stands

withered and browned, the idea
of time simply passing along the edges,
became the dust-slathered roadsides
ineffably streaming into view.

It was the selfless act of skinning an orange,
of emptying one's pockets into the day,
the day that passed quietly and without much
to go back to – it was this that you remade
unquestioningly and furiously within
your never-resting mind: as if in anger

you struck against your sense of things
as they must be, as they are
bound to be in the very end,
when the trees will stand in bloom,

when a figure you have met and forgotten
will return and demand what he is owed.

ABJECT FEAR

I shall make the sun set at noon
and bring darkness to earth on a bright day.

No sooner would the noon approach –
the specious lodestar sits in the pines.
One drunken sailor abets the frieze:
approaching in the dark these bare feet

must recall somehow their cunning.
One should have had a mind like that of
D'Artagnan – noble, yet hollowed out
by winter and the proud antics of Maurice.

Instead one is in one's penultimate trunks.
Nothing left to do. Nothing left to see.
One is at the end of one's simplicity –
the day dropping like a hawk, a thundering of hours

trailing us through sleepless nights.
I should have broken this hereafter;
the stench of the leaves astounds me.
There is only the noon. It is here and never ends.

COME WITH US

Secure in introspection
he peers at the watery pillars of his reflection.

Bishop

Such lights as I have seen
beaten on the prow: those ships
twitching on the wave. Soon, out
of distances recalling sleep,

I shall walk closely in these streets,
closer to the world I saw beneath
the dim lights of a battered sky.
I shall have small reason to complain;

not the hare nor the peacock
shall disturb me as I lie
deeply within the hold of my ship.
The fish shall not disturb me,

the clipper and the sable shall pass
along the white edges of my view.
The women who toil at the sails
shall shake me and speak

to me as I recall my name:
'Come with us and see the sea,
it knows that you are here. It falls
again and again for you.'

ON BEING THE PALE ORNITHOLOGIST

It is this simple matter of defining
whatever moves beyond those pines and birches.
As though their speckles were the finest
forms of conceiving light: amongst themselves –
flashings of sunlight, amass of birds.
Speaking of trees, these moments seem
their own procession: here fades a memory
of you withdrawing like smoke through the pines.
In fact there are few things like this moment
when the birds lift up their heavy heads,
and the unmoved proprietor of sleep, being
of course the red-breasted goose or the finch
leaning closely to her mate, at long last
stops to consider these restless shores.

He, Thomson, was not always of this shining
disposition. Sunlight frightened him,
as did his own reflection, mirrored in the night,
whenever he would stumble out to meet it.
The birds seemed busy with their own conjectures,
having also to adjust to their observer,
much as seeing a thing will leave it open
to its seeing you – to looking away and returning
to the line you had long forgotten you were reading
before the birds appeared, before
these endless nights among the pines
became the tilt and the motion of the light.

*

BENJAMIN NEHAMMER is a writer and translator from Copenhagen, Denmark, where he lives with his wife, Minna, and his son, Jacob. His work has previously appeared in *SSYK* and *PN Review*.

The poems in this selection contain eighteen different species of animal – more than I would have guessed before I sat down to count them. I can't explain the presence of so many animals beyond saying that I like them and always have. It might reflect a desire for strange worlds and lives outside my own experience, and an interest in the ways in which it's impossible to disentangle the human from the natural world. The strangest animal of the eighteen is the barreleye fish in 'Baby Swimming'. This species has a transparent head and tubular, upward-facing eyes designed to detect prey swimming above. It seemed a suitable creature to represent the odd experience of attending a baby swimming class as a non-parent.

Several of the other poems address issues of uncertainty, choice and the future, especially with regards to choosing whether or not to become a parent. 'Swimming Between Islands' was written in response to a tweet by a man asking how women will spend the years from ages 40 to 80 if they don't become mothers. The tweet prompted a surprisingly beautiful thread full of people without children listing the things they plan to do with their lives.

New places, real and imaginary, sparked many of the poems. 'At the Cathedral of the Spilled Blood' was written after a year studying Russian in St Petersburg. 'Clean White Bones' followed a visit to a pirate supply store in San Francisco which contained an aquarium and a sign banning marriage proposals. 'At Mirror Lake' was written during a trip to Yosemite National Park in California.

'Hervör and Völund' was also inspired by Yosemite. A grove of giant sequoias seems an unlikely place to set an Old Norse myth, but there was something about the heat, the circling turkey vultures, and the prescribed burning practices used in the forest that felt right for the story of a magical blacksmith. It is told from Hervör's perspective – she is only briefly referenced in the sources, a valkyrie who was married for seven years to Völund (known as Wayland the Smith in Anglo-Saxon tales).

Writing poetry, for me, has always felt like treading a fine line between clarity for the reader and the creation of emotion and atmosphere during the reading experience. How far can you compress the poem before it becomes unintelligible? My favourite poems create an atmosphere that can be gleaned almost before reading – the images shine out from single words and short phrases, from the shapes and gaps on the page. I like poems that are almost places in themselves – places you can return to again and again and find something new each time.

*

SWIMMING BETWEEN ISLANDS

The island you were born on
is crammed with cabinets
and grandfather clocks.

Nearby, the island of children
with its shrieks and red tapestries
and the island of *one day, when*.

You have the sea and its bed,
a silvery current of hair
and a necklace of eggs

where a hundred new things grow.
The horizon looks toothed
but those are more islands:

the island of slow translation,
the island of choirs. An island of frogs
who spend their lives inside flowers.

On some you'll find you breathe better
underwater than in their thundery air.
Soon you'll have an island forest,

ribcage ferns exhaling green.
Swimmers will come to your house
to borrow your eyes.

DIVINATION

We knew everything, playing oracle on the carpet.
Saturdays crawled with our ladybird circus –
from the ends of our fingers, solemn as blood,
   we sent them to find our future husbands.
We let them trickle down
   our wrists into the birdbath
to see if they'd keep walking while we drowned them,
jealous of their easy flight

   from one shape to the next.
Now, like hanged men, we want to buy futures
and there's someone doing tarot at the end of Brighton Pier.
   Stars are poking holes in the sky.
      There's an airy clatter

   of cards falling into place
but stranger things are happening beneath our feet:
coppers chink through the boards

onto rows of starlings
stacking themselves like decks, noisy as a masked ball.
   We think *fluke* has something to do with wings
then remember whales, gliding
         despite the weight of all they know.
We watch the stragglers find their place under the pier,
   all the sea's dark spread ahead of us.

SURVIVORS

Aunts drink tea for hours – they have no mirrors or clocks
but each other's faces tell the time.

Why do their hands shake and rattle the cups in their saucers?
We prowl the flat – the hallway dark with years of coats,

the dining room with carpets on the walls.
Each visit we think something will be different

but there's always the same red View-Master
with unchanging views of Prague, and no TV.

We draw elaborate tunnels and hold funerals for bees;
the cheese plant grows towards the window.

Our aunts show us a glass case of curled-up figures.
All we want is the china cockatoo and toy koalas.

Their arms come towards us lined with numbers –
we wriggle away from their touch.

BABY SWIMMING

My friend and I each take a twin
into the pool – when we dip them
they come up laughing,
lashes spiked like urchins.

I am not their mother,
I don't know the words to these songs.
Surprising how hard it is
to hold the slippery egg
of his belly as he kicks and kicks

propelling us round this aquarium.
We're breathing bleachy steam
with strangers passing by and glancing in.
Am I holding him wrong?

I am that fish with a see-through head
and all its machinery on show –
tubes pulsing, bulbous green eyes
scanning up to the light –
we hardly know what all the parts are for.

CLEAN WHITE BONES

Two cuttlefish are waving
in their glassy world
as I go to hold your hand.
Our fingers clash

and I wonder
if it's any easier for them,

with twenty legs to tangle,
six hearts to please.

They speak a patterned language
of moody stripes and flashes,
the signs of love imprinted
on their skin,

leave their eggs
like a dropped necklace,
ruffled versions of themselves
suspended in each blackened bead.

I shift and break our grasp,
thinking of the jewel you offered,
of all their hearts
and our half-hearted kisses.

If we could take their place
there'd be no mess,
just our children in the weeds
brightening like bulbs.

AT MIRROR LAKE

It took us by surprise, how fast the moon rose –
a stone thrown from the cliff

floating loose in hot blue sky.
We asked why, as if its grey bloom

in the day was extraordinary.
Our words clipped, unkind with fatigue.

I watched your profile – the suddenly unfamiliar
curve of your nose. We thought we knew

how things like day and night
and love would work.

I held you too hard, my nails
made chilly little moons along your arm.

AT THE CATHEDRAL OF THE SPILLED BLOOD

Tserkov' Spasa na Krovi, St Petersburg

We buy eggs   painted with the silence of snow
scarves wrapped tight   around our mouths
Ice crystals prickle our noses   when we breathe

Mum's hiding the vodka from granny   in a high cupboard
She arrives in a red fur coat   a basket of freshly baked buns
the smell of nutmeg and cabbage

The men have eyes red from drink   as they tell us again
the story of the sack   the car boot   the journey south
They stand at the edge of the room   like grandfather clocks

Baby sister is in her cot   wise old face turned
from a single piece of birch   We carry her inside us
sisters   mothers   grandmothers

wrapped in coats and scarves   until we're round as matryoshka dolls
lined up at the market   beside the painted eggs
Our steps grow louder   the farther we are from home

the darker it gets among the trees
When a car pulls up to the kerb   my boots bite the ice
like a clenched jaw   the glass winds down with a hiss

Devushki   he's saying   *Sing for us!*
Of course you can sing   pretty girls like you
and I'm not sure if it's him   or granny speaking now

We're weaponised and vitreous   ponytails brittle with frost
Under our coats   our hip bones slice our lilac jeans
The men are out of the car   blocking the pavement

Granny's hanging the eggs   in the window
Their glitter's more real   than the street outside
the red dots might be us   in the snow

BALLOONIST

Haworth Gala, 1906

She is wet to the waist
in river, a minnow girl
slipping through lanes,
always looking
for the ropes

somebody hangs
in the woods
near water,
or that feeling you get
at the edge of cliffs.

On the moors
the walls lose
their footing,
lurching up hills,
along scars.

She looks down on the village,
pictures it wilder –
black hats a penguin circus,
the Old White Lion
roaring her name –

all those extra hearts
to bloody her.
She chooses
the balloon's silky bones,
a lampfish sky.

LAST EGG COLLECTION

From here the sea
between stacks
is a green ribbon –

thick socks
and a horsehair plait
stop us plunging

down rock
white with seabirds,
laced with nets.

We fight the sword-beaks of gannets
for our snowy harvest
of eggs and feathers.

Below,
the empty houses
look like open graves.

PABBAY CLIFFS

Belly to grass,
greenish jelly sea
below. Here,
next to my face,
miniature worlds of moss:

tiny trees and stars,
near and far
as the queue of strangers
behind me
waiting their turn

to look down
at the guillemots
hidden by the cliff's
pleats, each precariously
at home.

O warm egg bodies,
the rocks look soft
enough down there,
greened with weed.

In the distance
killer whales,
fins tall as you.

INTO THE FJORDS

Someone's turned over
                a mirror, the grey-backed sea
                a polished image of the sky.

Waterfalls pour upwards,
                meeting themselves at the shore –
windows in pieces on the water,
                        sills waving –

whole villages submerged and shimmering.

Clouds hide a wreck,
            a ship's broken ribs, splintered

like this edge of land – leaning over
the bow, I see myself
capsized.

HERVÖR AND VÖLUND

I held the birds of myself together
for seven years.
When I left with his ring,
he made seven hundred

to tempt me back.
Offered earrings like green eyes,
brooches of milk teeth,
silver cups like small skulls.

I put our sky-blue eggs
beyond his reach,
up where distance
softened everything to feathers.

I loved his hands,
their blacksmith skill.
He loved black velvet bark
after a fire.

But it wasn't only metal he could shape.
Now he's far above me,
a vulture with black fingers
and a blood-drop head.

Our children's veins were green-lit –
young trees
with the smell of smoke
already in their branches.

*

CHARLOTTE EICHLER was born in Hertfordshire and lives in West Yorkshire. Her debut pamphlet, *Their Lunar Language*, came out in 2018 with Valley Press. Her poems have appeared in publications including *PN Review*, *The Scotsman*, *The Rialto*, *The Island Review*, *Stand* and several Emma Press anthologies. In 2017/18 she was a *Poetry London* mentee with Vahni Capildeo. She holds a BA in English Literature and Russian and an MA in Norse and Viking Studies, and works for the *International Medieval Bibliography* at the University of Leeds.

As a teenager I came across John Donne's perfect poem, 'The
Sun Rising'. I was captivated by its perspectival shifts, as well as
the casual, teasing subtleties of the speaker. Reading the poem
for the first time, it felt as if I had briefly time-travelled into
some seventeenth-century mental zone, disconnected from
the classroom I was sitting in. Ever since, I've enjoyed using
conceits, which a lot of the poems here, such as 'The Record
Feels The Needle', 'Plectrum My Ribs', and 'Cabling' employ.

Around this time, I also discovered that writing formal,
rhymed stanzas helped me find an objective space, an escape
from myself. Form and rhyme, then, and the tradition of craft,
and breaking apart forms are also of concern, something 'The
Fountain' particularly explores. Breaking apart traditional
form often feels like a chaotic reordering, an unconscious
intersection of image and sound. Nietzsche said 'music, at its
highest level, must also seek to attain its highest expression
in images'. Poetry is a balancing act, and we have to keep
smashing, then re-stringing the lyre.

Other poems are less concerned with form and tradition,
more about stalking an image or sensual appreciation. The
precision which is necessary when writing to a large extent
depends upon an imprecise state of mind. Asked about his
paintings, Bacon once commented that 'if anything ever does
work [...] it is in that moment when consciously I don't know
what I'm doing'. I feel similarly, but I would add that not
knowing must be heightened by a practised solitude.

Coming back to Donne, I find the special lightness peculiar
to certain Renaissance poetry fascinating. 'Humour' is too
general a word to describe it; perhaps it is a kind of wisdom, an
unseriousness which fools the tragic. In fact, cheer and foolery,
I think, are a necessary inoculation - or intoxication, against all
the darknesses of being a twenty-first-century human being.

The fool and the poet cannot be data-gathered or outwitted by algorithms: poetry, then, is for me also quiet rebellion. So whilst a number of poems here are despairing, others, such as 'Daft Cemetery', are jesting pieces too.

*

DAFT CEMETERY

There's something ivy at work,
a vast fuss which gets to whispering
amidst the rocks. Then crooked

to a fault, the path leads
down amongst the scrum
of crumbling graves and odd

plots with weeds. Picking
my way through, I can't keep
a straight face. Have to

laugh – blurt out
against nothing – trip
on a stray root scrabbling.

Words chip into silence.

It doesn't give.

Only light there is comes from a
mass of leaves – there –

he jests, a bird – a robin – hopping
branch to grave, and finding
death as much a lark as me.

I nod,
and follow him to
somewhere outer, lighter.

I walk out whistling.

THE FOUNTAIN

The fountain's quick transparent harp
is pulsing as I read. Each string
connects to light and loops unsharp
in splashy angles, slipped notes freed
to scatter over asphalt sparkling.

With shrieks and giggling, three kids
race through its music maze. They play
a sloppy circle with their hands –
they reconfigure, twist the spray
to spout scattershot, go haywire

across the pavement. I see
their pleasure is in breaking up
the lyre's shape. They discompose
its fine design, they chop and cup
each jet, reroute and split what flows

into a flashy wreck. Anarchists!
They dash the sequenced protocol,
obstruct the water's symphysis,
they flout control, force off course
with arms and legs the fountain's har-

mony. What rains here now is sheer
glow.

PLECTRUM MY RIBS

Do. Pilfer a penny.
Put it between these ribs.
Make them ring. Force
out the hollow they hold.

Go on. The penny's your
pick. So pluck me a song.
Stab at the empty. Tune
and strum my obsolete ribs.

Sing along. Strike up a
lick. Shake me. Thrum
where a heart once

FRIVOLITIES

See where they go, leaves,
    frivolities that flock, unfreeze
from stem to flit by city clock
stone-toned, then breezing step,
and sloping mock the plot
    we're standing on.

They seem to stop, but these
        surprise you cycling,
    splice your spoke, reel
where hurried folk walk
off. They make us pause,
take stock mid-dash – we watch
    them scattering, then shop
or scoot for rest.

Look how they fall, all ease
    and unforced flight, tipped
upwards spiralling – all light
and fearless flick – a levity
    that heeds no gravity,
a casual slip to where you sit,
bench-bound, struck
    by a complex trick – leaves, poof!
Pure foolery!

DEATH

Your signature is poppy,
red sprawl contrived to make
a grave less dull, a field

look taller. The sky falls
deep across your edge of dye –
or splatter through grass.

It's bitter, too. A full choke.
Puffed cheeks of thistle stars,
slope of weed, heights
that ask nothing.

THE RECORD FEELS THE NEEDLE

My hollow eye
watches the ceiling.
I stare and stare,
unable to think,
my mind uncoiling.

Who set me going?
Which hand first
pressed
in me this music?
This sound I can't stop.

I stutter glitches.
Scuffs, slips repeat.
Same old, same old,
same old song.

THE SYRUP'S IN THE SOUND

The maple leaves crunch best in frost.
All up our drive they've lain for weeks,
at first as purplish and airy heaps –
kick-upable, lightness still in them,
spiralized, shifted, dragged by gusts,
some hefted off to neighbour roads,
the rest left whispery and weightless,
in downpours going dark and shiny skinned.
One yellow one I saw had cupped the rain,
its brimful blurred migrations: moving cloud
that bloomed in wordless pass, held still
inside the leaf's thin grasp,
its grip a day or so to last before more wind,
more crazy rain smashed in its pool,
and with it parts of vein and margin lost.
All leaves were lessened into eaten silks.
In palm were almost nothing, thin as web,
ragged as Sapphic verse, fragmented skins.
Gold cells gone dark like blighted honeycomb.
The whole road browned, dulled with growing cold.
I'd go out late instead and pick out stars –
ones where the leaves had been – that shone, nestled
like fruits between the forks of maple roof.
Here were fires that carried on, brightness unshed.
From so much massed loss to these
I turned my thoughts –
forgot the path's compressed and muddied dank
until one week of January frosts;
then walking down the road, not listening
at first, I came to hear its tonic crisp.
Like breaking sugar lumps. Each crunch
a maple leaf – hoar-edged, blade stiff with ice –

that cracked right through beneath my feet.
In that one sound I heard the summer's slow-soft voice –
its sweet preserved. Brought back to me green life
amongst the cold, the bare shadows of trunks.

RAGWORT, 1940

> *Out of the bomb craters during the Blitz bloomed ragwort, lilies of the*
> *valley, white and mauve lilac.*
>
> Peter Ackroyd, *London: The Biography*

Small hope of jazz, it
ups, decides on vertical,
brings with it such others --
such as these slim hymns to the sky:

homeosoma nimbella,
tyria jacobaeae,
thalera fimbrialis

It has the go-go gold of sax,
bravado major of a real town player,
solo 'whatever' whether earth
or sky collapse, cool rag regardless
of terror, blood, ash.

Ragwort opts, despite
everything, to come through.

ISLE

Isle of the Dead (3rd version, 1883), Arnold Böcklin

Why cypresses?
What is it in those thin shapes? And so
slim-dark against the cliffs
they come up like a sharp green fire,
an elven cunning to their wild tops.

What is it that strikes the spirit
as we contemplate that wood? Is it
that no light has snuck through? Or is it
the weirdness of its bent height? The fact
it grows above the rock, pillar-like, compelling
us to forge a path?

We're hooked to their dark authority,
their stern, impartial beauty. These are our judges
before the bone silence, the no-return.

I'VE DRUNK THE MALMSEY

I've drunk the malmsey twice.
And both times afterwards
have headed home – by way
of shore – have tripped
along the misty coast, the fresh
wind's salt a kind of cure.

Being no connoisseur,
I'd say it tasted as a rose.
Much layered

and replete with sugaring.
But something else – perhaps
a special silt or stone
got in and made it have this
deadly, this druggy nose.

It's shattering! Bedevils
brain. Will hobble you,
has hobbled me. Tipsied.
Slipped me up my gait,
my mind speaks nonsense verily.

This particular malmsey –
a real palsy. A blueness
it brings. The stares and shakes.
Has had me tongue-slurred
roaming streets,
too much dawn in the eye. Still –
I hope to drain a third chance
                              – and quick.

CABLING

Laid down with roots, old
chips of jagged pottery, cut
glass, rust parts – it links
us. It worms through dead

grass, flint, tyre, bits of vase –
all the rubbish from last
century –
links us through all of this.

Just lately, though, I've
heard a glitch your end.
Some unspeakable slur,
slight static errrrr
that lingers when you speak.

I've put it down to the line's
old lisp. But weird it is. Goes
tinselly after certain words. Myth
is almost mix, and
love most gravelly – gruff,

it's like a faulty kiss,
as if the wires' rough tssssk
were part conspiracy. As if
the ground below were
listening.

It's getting worse. Last night
I hardly heard a word you said.
Began to think the breaking
up was in my head. That

really it's all neural jam.
Botched line psychology.
An error pre-installed so
things will always fray, spark wrong.

One day, I might skip all
of this. I might just spade
the whole mapped thread.
Axe it. And never mind.

MEANWHILE... WE DIG

So love would not. Give.
Budge? No. Nope. Would not

lift a faint eyelid or even
let me draw a chancy lot.

So all was left, I thought, was dig.
Dig straight down where the old
roots sleep, and find there, at least,

communal rot. And I did.
Slid my bones to the charnel
plot and lay where the skeletons keep.

I really did. Put my tongue
where the worm hair wigs, and the
skull is a cracked crockpot.

And I thought I would never return.
But I did. Through the coffin's lid
and the earth I came back up.

And I learned to live, and not mind love.
When it's gone just dig, dig, dig.
And never stop.

*

NELL PRINCE lives in Lincolnshire and has had poems
published in various magazines including *PN Review*, *Perverse*
and *Measure*. She was runner-up in the 2016 Jane Martin
Prize, and in an email sent in 2013, Harold Bloom described
the poem she sent to him as 'authentically promising'.

I love when images clash. When an image describes something perfectly but seems to have barrelled in from outside this particular poem, bringing a whole new set of luggage. I love these collisions and moments of discord because they make connections beyond what's rational. For me, this is at the heart of poetry. I never set out to write a poem knowing where it will end (what would be the point of writing if you did?) It's through image-making I discover new ways of understanding and articulating what I have been carrying around with me.

Of course, I comb through the initial drafts and move the tangle from my notebook (or my phone's voice recorder) onto a computer screen. I worry at it and make decisions about what should be grown or cut. If you're going to ask a reader for their time, something they won't get back, you should be giving your time too. But I'm not transcribing something I've already seen; I'm drafting a communication to myself as well as to a reader.

These poems were written during the disturbing end-years of the 2010s. In 'Early Winter' readers may recognise *FiveThirtyEight*, a blog known for accurate election predictions. The night before the 2016 USA election it predicted Hillary Clinton had a 71% chance of winning. At the time *The New York Times* predicted an 85% chance of a Clinton win, *Huffington Post* 98%, *Predict Wise* 89%, *Princeton Election Consortium* 99%, *Daily Kos* 92%. By the time this anthology is published there may be a new president in the White House, but the concerns of these poems are sadly no less pressing. We are still 'charged with shifting the axis of the earth'.

*

HOUSEKEEPING

While scrubbing saucepans, gloved hands
sucked and sunk in steamy waters,
I've not looked up and caught the blushing tail
of an epiphany through the kitchen window.
Or glanced one floating in the burnished flank
of a toaster. A child next-door is practising scales
on an angry block-nosed recorder.
Small woman. Sensible pebbledash.

Can we not be honest with one another?

Is it really just me who must shove
all the mess in a cupboard
for the whole afternoon
to get nearly anywhere?

Come, take my hand, walk with me while the dam holds.
The downstream path is in festival.
I know a pub where we'll meet such characters.

WATCHING A NORTH AMERICAN LOON FROM ST THOMAS' HOSPITAL

It mainly solves its problems
by not being there at all
but under water, coming up
in the smallest surface stiches.

I'm in a four-bed ward
and one of us just died.
They've closed the curtains
and sent in chatty students
with packets of digestives
to keep our minds away
from the removal.

So, I decide, that,
down there, is the descendent
of a North American Loon.
Look how it loops
under the white tourist cruiser.

In Alberta, a single pair
could rule a lake
the size of Westminster.

Here, her polka dot coat
is gravy stained with Thames water.

Any second,
she will shoot her call like a flare
and it will hang
over the office workers of Whitehall.

THREE KING CANUTES

The king, his gold retainers, a school of priests,
the men who can't remove their helmets
out of doors, and the plush unarmored
trudge a mirror-surfaced beach.

1

Laugh, laugh at the foolish fop-haired
Rollo square-face as he waves his sword,
slashes water, cold stung, face infection-hot
with tears, a mug in ruined boots.

2

The second king has quietness: a loved teacher
waiting for his class to own their error.
Surf nuzzles at his ankles.
This man's immovable, except a roll of hair
caught in the wind's chill currents and his eyes
resting in the eye of each advisor
until the sycophant wilts.

3

This last Canute has brought a camera crew.
His open suit and tie flap, the one concession
his women swapping heels for ballet pumps.
When water fills his shoes, it doesn't matter
he is rich and there's blankets in the waiting SUV.
He roars the waves will hold
as water's licking up his trouser legs.

He thinks he's in a story
and the better story wins.
That truth is just the story
that the audience lets in.

It doesn't matter if he's Cnut or Canute,
if we're in Norfolk or in Neverwhere.
He's miked up, entertaining
and his wife's and daughter's hair
is sprayed as hard as bronze,
the wind, the sea, cannot mar the shot.

SOOTHSAYERS

The volcano's in its third trimester,
our soil bulges over elbowing fire.

So fling open the airing cupboard,
let's dress in the bed sheets:
we're online posting as soothsayers from Pompeii
searching new ways to say the same dire warnings.

O, the iced deliciousness of being ignored
by everyone, except for anyone we know.
Which is not to say,
we don't wipe a thin sulphur dust
from our phone-screens as we read.

*

You've seen the casts from Herculaneum:
human ice-pops.

We thought we knew them
but X-rayed this spring
we learned 'The Beggar'
had a young man's hips
and a bronze buckle
coagulated inside.

                    *

Filtering is in its infancy.
The next generation of wearables
will allow you to live in a curated city.
You'll see your friend alone in the street
among a shoal of infectious shadows.

SLAUGHTER ON ASHBY LAKE

Blackflies thick as showers of rice –
mosquitos pitched their rigs and drilled
a mess of extra knuckles on my hands.
My morning shower was torture,
the lightest drizzle
sprung a hundred clock alarms.

That May in Canada, I was a sack of blood
hauled round for scrums of butchers
with dirty electric knives.
I wore ligatures, red lines across my wrists,
my waist, ankles where I pulled draw-strings
too tight. Nothing was sealed.

I wore a veil, dislocated my sight, I'd slip focus
between the lakeshore and my grill.

I tried sprays with puns: buzz-off,
smidge. I trawled the forums for hacks
(*try Goji Berry Skin So Soft*). I used Deet
until I didn't know if the deepening red
was from the open-wounds or chemicals.
I spread on cooling lotion like cream cheese.

Once, I blinked and caught one in my lash.
As I picked it out, the mangled parts still buzzed.

They pocked the surface of the lake like rain
and when the storms did come they didn't care:
thunder was God tearing open another pack
of biting things to get at me.

Then, at the end of May, they hatched:
a shiny guard, ballista-bodied dragonflies,
helicopter gunships thick as thumbs
and matchstick musketeers in dandy blue.
I'd never thought to google what they ate
until, within a week, they'd cleared the air.

THE ENGLISH SUMMER

Dun-coloured endangered species of specialist interest;
best found on grungy paths, behind gabardines,
near shoes on school radiators, wet socks at work.
A furred creature, hood-hidden, brolly-blinded, shy.

The invasive species: a fearsome firestorm
of peeled blue sky. Allelopathic leaf-crisper,
river-fading grass-bleacher, ice-cream-smiling
skin-killer, furze-burning-forest-eater, agricide.

See the burn blisters on the ridge of this ear.
See water rationing. See heat edema. See dizziness.

THE DEATH OF A FRIDGE

Poured on skin, lighter fluid
burns shallow. My hand in flames
was no worse than a plaster ripped off;
we were more burnt by the sun.

I can't even remember his name.
He had a newspaper rolled in a torch
burning up too quick
and nowhere to drop it,
so we slammed it in the fridge.

The box sealed. The rubber trim
sucked tight. We couldn't force it
anymore than we could pull apart
a dinner plate. Not crack a dish
but hold the rims and pull it in two,
everything has its own way to break.

The air was eaten: a dimple
in the cool enamel, a crease,
then, drawn from the inside,
the whole white weight crumpled

with thunks of deep struck metal,
as a girl, trapped by an earthquake,
might smash keys on a pipe
when she still thinks of rescue.

EARLY WINTER

It's not a frozen spoon on your tongue.
It's a mildew eating everything;
the path through the forest is pulp.

The trees weigh up the bad choice
and send a shunt to amputate each leaf.
A cataract ripens on the surface of the sun.

Still, the moss is more inviting now,
soft spires; we could curl down like mites.
The river flexes currents on its surface.

These assertions can be verified by anyone
with a car, or the leisure to daytrip by train,
or a little wood protected by a local council.

We're used to waiting winter out
like a debilitating cold. Our faith in spring
so strong we'd never call it faith.

It's statistical analysis: every year we lived,
that year it came. These things can be predicted.
We read *FiveThirtyEight*. We know it comes,

it must. Or we're stood in rotting undergrowth,
ankle deep in muck with mittened hands
charged with shifting the axis of the earth.

A STONE WALL AROUND A DUKE'S PARK IN 2019

You didn't think a private wall could be so long.
It cuts through thin-grass sheep fields,
clay-clubbed lulls, into cattle streams,
past thunderclouds of gorse.

After three uphill miles, you find a door
with a jagged hole the size of your hand.
You can't resist pressing up to see:
more moor, more heather, a few black birch.

What you can't know is the wall from the other side.
What the Duke could've painted,
perhaps a seaside board with a fat-thin couple
and an oval for your face?

What do your hands look like from over there?
What speech balloon slips tail-first into your mouth?

LADY GODIVA

It's lucky she has hair like frothy seaweed
that rolls around the sea like it is hair
but now she's standing naked in the courtyard

it sticks to skin like swathes of sweated chard
so her genitals are shielded by damp greens.

Her horse has also exited the picture
and she's quietly stepping off the mounting block.
If all of Coventry will turn their backs
and focus on the whitewash down the walls,
or painted cloths if they are burgher's daughters,
or crusts of daub if they are bootless poor,
then she doesn't really need to ride the horse
and anyway the beast is flint and muscle
with a bag of broken knuckles in its mouth.

Later she will learn where Peeping Tom lives
and use a hatpin on him while he sleeps.

GREEN MAN IN SPRING

There's something in my teeth,
a thread of cress? A beansprout?
I have the urge to cough, little
chuffs, an engine failing to catch
growing to a dark wet hack

until I'm bent clutching my thighs
choking up a swell in my throat.
I hook my finger in and pull
a damp wad of pondweed,
hair from a plughole,

when I feel a kind of worm,
probe up under my tongue

and I can see it just under my nose
white, flailing. I try to rip it
but it's like thick plastic, it stretches

turning green, then pops up leaves
easy as umbrellas, heart shaped bindweed
crawling up my face, my ears
over my forehead and as I reach
I feel the crown's white megaphone blooms.

HOW TO BALANCE LAW BOOKS
ON YOUR HEAD

The problem isn't how, I absolutely know
the answer is to go to a Main Street
some town I don't live and find a stranger
who hates me, and my clothes, and my voice
and who (while they would never dream
of hurting me in person) suspects
the world would be better with me dead,
and persuade her that she wants to stand
so close my greasy nose presses into hers
and, recycling each other's soupy breaths,
balance the books between us on our foreheads.
My only problem is how to do *that*.

*

HOLLY HOPKINS grew up in Berkshire, grew up even more in London and now lives in Manchester. Her debut pamphlet, *Soon Every House Will Have One*, won the Poetry Business Pamphlet Competition and Poetry Book Society Pamphlet Choice. Holly has been an assistant editor of *The Rialto*. She has received an Eric Gregory Award, a Hawthornden Fellowship and was shortlisted for the inaugural Women Poets' Prize.

Acknowledgements –
Early Winter – *Poetry News*
Soothsayers – *Poetry London*

An ice cube may appear mundane at first glance, but transport it to Bronze Age Crete and it comes alive with a whole new world of connotations: it transforms into a luxury, a logistical extravagance. Who gets to consume this rare commodity, what deals have they struck to acquire it and with whom, and what ends will they go to in order to retain it? Would I strike these same deals and go to those same ends? I love how a historical consideration of an object unearths new dimensions, textures and economies within it.

Objects carry these histories, but as we encounter and consume and make use of them in everyday life, these myriad significances collapse into a singular functional role. This mirrors our experience of words and language. Almost every word contains a legion of potential connotations and usages but of necessity we collapse these into something approaching a singular meaning when we speak in order to communicate. When we read on Twitter that a company has liquidated its assets, we understand this as information relating to finance and do not picture the assets literally melting into a puddle. Poems offer a space to coax meaning and significance from language, to extend them past the point of immediate, pragmatic collapse. I love poems which strike a balance between what sounds (relatively) inconspicuous to the ear but also where the deeper suggestions of the language are just beginning to break through to the surface.

Like objects, words have their own histories and I often lose hours going down the rabbit hole of etymological dictionaries. Recently, while attempting to write a poem about a windmill, I was fascinated to discovered that the *m-l* in mill is the same *m-l* in molar and the same *m-l* in maelstrom; all deriving from a root **mele* meaning to crush or grind. For me, part of the joy of writing a poem is playing these fossilizations within the language off against the living, breathing connotations we create for the words as we go about living our lives.

I write poems because (like anyone else) I have strong feelings about the things I experience and witness, and (like anyone else) I have a strong desire to justify those feelings to myself. When I read poems it is because I want to feel something, some connection to another person, some sense that my own human experiences are out there in the world and some image of them will be mirrored back to me. When I write a poem, it is, at its heart, an attempt to make another person feel something. It has the kind of charged sensation of getting something off your chest; of telling something you hadn't realised you were holding back; of saying the hard things like 'I'm scared' or 'I'm sorry' or 'I'm grateful', which I suppose are all kinds of variations on the theme of 'I'm here'. Or, even, *something*'s here.

*

GNOMON

Because light
is in the habit
of recurring,
and even suns
must be subject
to the elasticity
of their routines;
because photons
plot their lives
through regular
traceable arcs –

there's a living
to be made
standing still,
hands in pockets,
making places dark.

DAEDALUS SAILS TO CRETE

Desperate to get south, I accept the king's commission.
On the black-sailed ship, I stew in my cabin, nauseous,
and ignore the captain's well-intentioned advice
to come up into the air and stare at the horizon.

Out of tact, that first night, I keep my eyes lowered
when his majesty raises his voice to cow his daughters.
The queen is icy. Her awful son makes an off-colour joke
and my scalp prickles as I sense him weigh my reaction.

In the morning, left to my own devices, I sit on the porch
and drink orange juice and sparkling water in the sun.
Ice is hauled down from the mountains in great dwindling blocks.
It hisses in my glass like a palace coup.

I understand now how, exactly, I'm a coward.
And how little it has taken to endear to me walls and ditches
and barriers of any kind, and of ever increasing convolution.
I understand now the king is an excuse. This was always inside me.

THE AMERICAN WAKE

When money was scarce, travel slow and perilous, illiteracy widespread,
and mail service highly uncertain and destinations only vaguely perceived,
the departure to North America of a relative or neighbour represented as
final a parting as a descent to the gravel.

K.A. Miller

It had all the mundanities
of truly significant events:

clearing the front room of dust,
a quick inventory of cups, saucers,

other quiet emblems of normality
pitching themselves suddenly forward

as from the background of a painting,
taking on a new, terrible solidness.

And then again, moments
when he felt something begin to swell

like the ripe side of a hill
he'd only just noticed was always there.

Invitations were clipped and embarrassed
and soon digressed to easier talk

of harvest, health or courtship.
One neighbour met him at the gate

as though to keep a ghost
from the threshold of a living home.

And they waked him –
with furniture pushed against the walls,

the room made strange with space;
with scraps of fond advice

pieced together in hushed tones;
with all the ache and memory muscle retains

of grief and grief's recurring motions –
they waked a living man.

Because even though there is a difference
between being dead and leaving,

there is a likeness between dying
and being somewhere that isn't here.

THE JEANIE JOHNSTON, 1855

The fine coppered and copper-fastened bulk
measures up to all the advertisements.
Seven-hundred tons of burden, crouched in harbour,
ready for the great plié and open ocean.

Each inch of rigging accounted for, coiled
and stowed or already high above everything,
loosed and swinging between the masts,
through air and evaporated salt crystals.

A crowd of people huddle up into a stubby queue
exchange a particular kind of currency:

doctor aboard – always finds clear weather –
lucky – lit a candle – write letters – you'll be fine –

Beyond the ship, rock pools shine under the sun,
a rich sardonyx burnished by sea water.
On the dock, they've unloaded the last of the cargo:
red and yellow pine timber from America and Quebec.

TRANSCRIPTION OF A KEEN

It couldn't have been easy getting it to lie flat on paper.
That's obvious from the asterisks.

Above the notes on the stave are some bizarre annotations:
Sobbing. Hand clapping. A kind of shake.

It's impossible to guess how they might fit into the music.
I can't read it well enough to get any real feel for the tune –

just enough to recognise the stranger movements.
There are parts where it breaks down to only two notes

going up and down and up from quaver to semiquaver.
A part in the middle accelerates to the point of nonsense

and I'm wondering as I look at it if this is just noise.
I'm almost certain it's unsingable.

In small letters along the bottom someone has written
och, och, och in embarrassed cursive script.

A final note in Italian says how loud the piece should be.

FIZZ

This preposterous
bottom-up approach:
mixing fungus
into wet and powder;

with time and proofing
it eats itself large,
comes alive,
devours its sugars

and doubles in size,
must be knocked,
then stretched, folded,
made elastic and smoother

so hooks of gluten
may snag together
in the kneading,
net themselves

in anticipation
of high temperatures,
effervescence,
transfiguration.

THE STOVE

When he looked at it he realised the fuse
box must have caught fire briefly because
the switches had all melted into thick
plastic blobs and there was an acidic
discolouration about the edges.
This meant no cooker, no kettle. The fridge
would have to be kept shut to keep the cold
in. The landlord was hard to get a hold

of – instead, he emptied cans of Pepsi
into the sink, carved them up carefully,
punctured neat holes in them with a corkscrew
and poured in a bright purple ethanol.
Denatured, undrinkable, it burned blue
and cooked beans and tea with a tang of metal.

WEBBING

what would you say
if it turned out
i was a giant
mechanical
spider who
didn't really
like the things we
both said we liked

if on further
inspection you
were to discover
my insides were
chock-full of
counterfeit silk
and i hated
your friend lisa

what if my gums
concealed big steel
fangs needed to eat
that retracted
seamlessly
that envenomed
that were very
much part of me

i hope that you'd
take a step back
think rationally
try to see things
as seen from
my perspective
hung upside down
from the ceiling

REAL TREE

my nana told me how my aunt
got allergies one year suddenly
from the christmas tree

how she took steroids for a week
to no avail in hopes of keeping
a real tree in her living room

she had to give up at 3am
on the 24th when it came down
to authenticity or breathing

she slipped out to the supermarket
open all night for christmas
and got a flat-packed tree instead

i can't stop imagining her doing the swap
the silent undecorating
the indignant ornaments on the floor

temporarily
i can't stop being impressed
by this colossal sleight of hand

the next morning my aunt asked her family
if they noticed anything different
and her husband panicked and said she looked nice

it was almost new year's
when he took out the vacuum
and noticed there were no pine needles

TO MY MOTHER AT MY AGE

while the bubble still glistens like a weekend away
and each year of the nineties sits on the calendar
in front of you like a fat promise
and both your parents are alive and around the corner

and in the papers and the magazines and on the weather
the threat of nuclear annihilation has subsided
to the point where you can start buying garden furniture
and speaking candidly to your doctor about sex

drive west to the fuchsia and the holiday homes
where on hot late nights you are implored
by friends and strangers alike to sing and sing and sing

because the icecaps are melting
and xtravision despite its robust complexion
will liquidate its stock and eventually cease trading

*

CONOR CLEARY is from Tralee, Co. Kerry and lives in Belfast. His work has appeared in *The Tangerine, Poetry Ireland Review, The Stinging Fly* and *Virginia Quarterly Review*. In 2018 he was the winner of the Patrick Kavanagh Award. His debut poetry pamphlet, *priced out*, was published by The Emma Press in 2019.

Translating Catullus has been, for me, like cage fighting with two opponents: not just A Top Poet, but the schoolgirl I was, trained to show the examiner that she knew what each word meant.

Then there's the referee. In the introduction to his honest translation, *The Poems of Catullus* (OUP), Guy Lee writes: 'There is surely no point in adding yet another to the number of free translations or paraphrases, however lively.' Yet here are my versions jostling with the rest. The trouble is that Catullus's tormented intelligence and romantic versatility make him irresistible. But in order to approach him I had to find out where he was, which took decades.

It eventually happened at a fetish venue in South London, The Flying Dutchman – an echo of Catullus's doomed obsessive love? Someone at life class, knowing I like a drawing challenge, had told me about a Japanese rope bondage (*shibari*) club called Bound. I asked the management if I could draw there; on arrival I was treated like the Queen Mother. Best of all, the schoolgirl was too young to be let in.

Before you get carried away, rope bondage people are dismissed as train spotters by the rest of the fetish community because of their nerdy devotion to knots. I've found a similar sense of acceptance and dedication around the tea urn at Kensington Gardeners' Club.

But as I became absorbed in drawing the emotional dynamic of performance in ink, with feathers, coffee stirrers, bamboo, oiled hemp bondage rope, the tip of a white man's dreadlock and actual pens, I found context, metaphor and idiom for Catullus – whom one could glibly define as a bisexual switch from the late Roman Republic when such concepts were meaningless: a stern moralist who splits into an anxious bitchy dominant with the boys, a howling sub with his nemesis, the older glamorous married woman he calls Lesbia (here called Clodia, which might have been her real name).

The flow of power between dominant and submissive is key to Catullus and to this bondage discipline. French rope star Gorgone – who does indeed leave men in various states of petrification – points out that being a top (someone who ties) is about humility; being a bottom is where true power lies.

I sometimes slipped through the floorboards to draw a club which met in the dungeon below the rope anoraks and catered for a different clientele, but Catullus would have been at home here too. Again, the management approved: 'She sits there like a little mouse, and gets us.'

I had another lucky break. I discovered that even as an alumna, or mere ectoplasm, I could seek permission to attend a Catullus textual criticism class at Oxford. The two professors in charge, Stephen Harrison and Stephen Heyworth, kindly allowed me to glimpse what was happening at the coal face. Apart from scattered quotations in others' works, Catullus's remaining poems were transmitted via one corrupted manuscript, now lost, so scholars are on an endless quest for authenticity. I wanted to peer closely at the meaning even though, while some of my versions hug the shore of the text, most of them plunge into choppy waters.

Here I offer two of the speculative readings. In poem number 56, was the boy alone or with a girl? And in number 101, nineteenth-century philologist Jacob Maehly speculated that Catullus wrote *amoris* ('of love') instead of *mortis* ('of death').

Finally, I owe a debt to the notes in Professor Kenneth Quinn's edition of the text. When I can't even work out what part of speech something is, he's on it.

*

CATULLUS: SHIBARI CARMINA

VII

Stress-testing are we, Mistress?
How many of your tropes in rope
Can be endured before the poet chokes?

Ply me hemp silk jute and tie me
Ichinawa, takate kote,
Futomomo, hishi karada,
Tasuki, kannuki,
Hashira, daruma shibari.
All of it. Semenawa for the burn.

Count the stars that spy on sly
Lovers when the night is ball-gagged –

That's how many of your tight knots and rope marks
Will deliver me beyond madness –
More than a voyeur's torch could spot
Or a jealous sensei take to pieces.

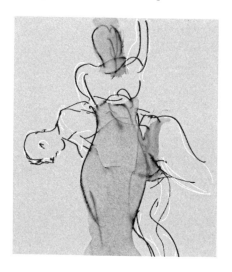

X V I

Beware the mighty sodomite face-bandit
(Me). You two batty-boys dishing out lit crit
Insist my kissy-fit verse is Hello Kitty.

Look, being the guardian of what's good
Is work for the poet, not for the poet's works.

Liberation from your taste police
Gives my words a musky allure that can stir

Not just boys but the prick-memory
Of shaggy old ex-shaggers.

So writing kiss poems is an unmanly feat?
First line, repeat. XX

X X X V I I

You boys queueing outside Berlin Berlin –
You think you're the only ones with cocks,
Let in to fuck the girls
While the rest of us get herded away?

Have another think.

*The poet fantasises about ejaculating in the reluctant faces of two
hundred male clubbers. He then considers his options.*

I'll squirt correctly spelt obscene graffiti
All over your façade

Because the girl who broke away from my hold –
Loved with more love
Than other women will reap,
The one I had such brutal fights to keep –
Is your house dominant.

They all want her, the cream of the alphas and –
Harder for me to bear – the bottom feeders

Especially *you*, lord of the hairy-arsed,
All the way from Saragossa's
Plague-zone of randy fluffy bunnies –
Señor Egnatius, raised to foreign nobility
By your clogged beard and glaring expat teeth
Scrubbed with vintage Spanish urine.

The poet puts down his tools and goes for a pee.

XXXVIII
...WITH A MURMUR... MY RAVINGS...

Can't go on but does
Can't be borne but must be
Down and the weight bears down
Each day each hour Cornificius
Bad for your Catullus
But have you written the least
The tiniest scrap to calm me?
Feel my rage. Is this all your love means?

Whisper me a consolation please
Sadder than Housman's trembling tears

LI

I can't compete with the rock-god superhero
God's begging him to take the shiniest halo
That man intent on you
Ogling provoking

Your sexy laughter I'm muted
My nerves torn out with hooks
Because when I see you Clodia I
Fumble for a line and

<*Find a lacuna*>

Mouth crammed with earth
Limbs hot and clumsy with longing
High tide pounding my skull

Trashed headlights and a windscreen
Crazed to opacity

Idling Catullus it stalls your intention
And maidens call it love-in-idleness
Without a plan you're restless and distracted
Idle coasting toppled kings and golden
Cities in legends

L I

Oh just go ahead with giving head to the godhead
God help us he outdogs the gods of dogging
Monopolising you with his cheap tactics
Paying attention

Making you laugh and my receptors go haywire
Because one look at you Mistress and
I can't even form a polite request
For *semenawa*

My tongue dries cold blue tied to bamboo
Slung body hurts in tight jute knots
Rope burns and bare skin flinches from hot wax drips
Techno rattles my brain
Stinging eyes
Submit to the blindfold and and

Wanking, Orlando. It's unproductive.
Wanking makes you fretful and distracted.
Legendary kings and shiny cities,
Lost to wanking

LVI

Oh you'll love this
Bloody hilarious
Cato yes no really
Don't go
Too funny
So I take some G
Sneak into the dungeon
On my own
Find a kid
Pounding some girl
I don't bother to ask
(So slap my wrist
It's a stupid rule anyway)
And make him the meat in the sandwich

Look, am I boring you or something
I bored him with this skewer lol
OK you can read it another way
It's dark and I'm dead
There was no girl
Just Mistress's boy slave
Beating time to thoughts of her as we do

Oh Christ look have some of this
Of course I can handle it

LVIII
GLUE. BIT.

Oh Caelius –

Mistress, Herself, her Worship, our own Lady of the
Labia, the one the poet loved
More than himself and all the rest –

Now downloadable dogging in urban areas
And choking on locally elected members

LX

You got your manners from scavenging mountain lions?
Or self-aborted from Scylla's horror-cave
To agitate the howling dogs lodged there?

Is that why you despise the beggar's
Plea of urgent need?

Your heat, your heart of a bitch.

L X X V

This is what we've come to, Clodia. My
Self-will has been dragged down by the beast in you and
Drowned in its own pool of meaning well.

I couldn't bring myself to like you now
Even if you played the convent girl

Or give up loving you, no matter how
Wide you spread your legs to the whole world.

C I

Flight-shamed through the earthbound ports and checkpoints
I'm here, my brother, for this bleak ceremony,
To help you fathom death's or love's assembly
And offer useless words to wordless ashes.
I wasn't strong enough to keep hold of you.
Now I'll never find the missing piece

Here are the conventional sad tokens
For the old rituals that told us so.
Take them sea-splashed with a brother's tears
And for ever like the tide, my brother,
I come to claim you and to let you go

*

ISOBEL WILLIAMS blogs about drawing and started live-drawing (depicting things as they happen) in 2011 when she was asked to draw under the A40 where it flies over Portobello Road. Other subjects have included Occupy camps and squats, performers preparing for the Notting Hill carnival, courtrooms, and Japanese rope bondage (*shibari*) performances and workshops in London, Oxford and Paris. Worlds collided for her when the Naked Rambler entered the dock at Winchester Crown Court.

In 2015 she drew the progress of *The Violet Crab*, Than Hussein Clark's cabaret-themed exhibition at the David Roberts Art Foundation in London. She has held solo exhibitions in London and Oslo, written articles, e.g. for *International Journal for the Semiotics of Law* and *The Amorist*, and given talks at law and humanities conferences in the UK and abroad.

She has had poems published in magazines, including *PN Review* and *Poetry Salzburg Review*, and been a runner-up in competitions, including *Stand* and the *TLS*.

She wrote and illustrated *The Supreme Court: a Guide for Bears* in 2017 and is contributing a chapter to *Design and Visualisation in Legal Education: Access to the Law*, published by Routledge in 2021. *Catullus: Shibari Carmina* is forthcoming from Carcanet in 2021.

My father died in 2010, my life forever divided into before and after. Dealing with his loss wrecked parts of myself I had constructed haphazardly, like the mask I had pressed to my face that I thought made me invincible, untouchable and mysterious. God help me, it slipped from my grasp, shattering at my feet like porcelain when he died, its pieces scattered all over. I felt raw and red. Less loved.

I have always written poetry but was afraid to commit to it, hiding behind writing about others' work. Death clarifies things, and now that my mask had smashed, I couldn't stop writing about my father. I grasped at snatches of memory, the intonations of his voice, his funny turns-of-phrase, so I could keep him here with me encased in the resin of my words. The poems from this period form part of my pamphlet, *White Whale* (Southword Editions, 2015).

Following its publication, I was struck by how ill-equipped and fragile I was when confronted with an event I could not control. I picked up the broken pieces of my mask and examined each one in turn. I cut myself many times but came to see how each sharp fragment formed part of a complex coping mechanism I had fashioned, a process which had begun when I was a child.

Back then, I had not made the connection between words and their multiple meanings – lamb in the field, *lamb for dinner*, chicken with chicks, *chicken and chips*. I wondered, and wonder still, what else I might have missed. Poetry then is an act of urgency for me; it provides an angle from which I can survey lacunae in my understanding, while its figurative elements supply material to generate a replica of my interiority. It is an act of conversion; I melt down my tempers into something molten to pour into the cracks.

Turning up the heat reveals that my concerns are, and not just as a writer, embedded in acts of consumption, replacement and resistance. For example, deciding to become a vegetarian at six, in hindsight, was an attempt at control but also a rebellion. I couldn't live with myself if my life depended on suffering and death; nor did I, even then, want to be judged as a woman. Such restriction is, as I found in my writing, a response to the paralysing fear of growing up, of sexuality, of death, and of shame, particularly as I come from an Irish Catholic background.

After *White Whale*, which felt both revelatory and a prelude, I started writing from the root of these anxieties. Reconstructing the shards of the broken mask conversely exposed the veracity of experience beneath. I fused these jagged pieces back together with words in my approximation of the Japanese art of Kintsugi or 'golden joinery.' Language allows for this. Poetry allows for this, and the poems took shape, text written to repair the fissures, to make something new, bolstered by the art and profound feminist anger of my poetry godmothers: Plath, Sexton, Olds, Clifton, Boland, Berry and Seuss among them.

Poetry created out of necessity resonates with me, written in the only way it could be written. The incendiary images of Sylvia Plath and the audacious truths of Anne Sexton, the assembled worlds of Emily Berry's books: their poems put things together to create shapes which engage and can be trusted. My poems are written in the only way I could write them – to be true. Among other things, they are a belated farewell to a difficult, extended girlhood and an embrace of a more complex – but I hope, healthier – womanhood. This journey didn't start until my world broke apart and that mask fragmented, but the funny thing is that my mask never really worked anyway. Everyone saw me, except myself.

SELFIE

Sitting alone in the house eating
my fingernails/watching the sky
move away. The room is full/versions of me
crouching on the floor/balancing on the window sill/
reclining on the pout of my lower lip/
asleep in the crease of my eyelid.
Not alone/with myself/A snare /I have been
running from   I do not live
the way humans are supposed to,
compare my face to others you know.
I fall short/an embarrassing fringe/No matter
what face I try on   it's exhausting.
All versions shake our heads.
There is much to do/until we think we are not
What We Are: Victoria(s). I see
those letters written on envelopes I know
are for me   because of the shape
of that word/that greedy V –
its two arms open wide/ready
to accept anything.

OPEN YOUR MOUTH

As a toddler,
     Krishna ate clay
          for fun,
               his worried mother
                    prying open his mouth
                         felt herself whirling in space, lost
                              inside that baby mouth

the whole universe,
moving and unmoving creation.
The earth, its mountains and oceans,
moon and stars,
planets and regions
and the child Krishna
with his wide-open mouth
and her kneeling
before him, and within
that mouth another
universe
and within
that mouth
another
universe
and within
that mouth
another
universe
and within
that mouth
another.

Eat,
he said, holding out
the mud
in his chubby hand,
and so on,
or we both starve.
She opened wide, kept
her tongue flat. The substance
was thick
and active.
She did not know

what she was
  tasting,
    she swallowed
      and felt
        full.

BEACHED WHALE

At first I thought that enormous lump of red-brown on the sand
was the trunk of some ancient, washed-up tree.

It was only when I mounted the object,
digging my small hands into something far too pliable,
that it really hit me, the stale smell of a thousand low tides

and the mute open mouths of the many onlookers
with their hysterical dogs, the seagulls circling like squalling clouds,
my mother's curlew scream as she ran towards me, disjointed.

Astride the whale like this,
looking at my mother move through dimensions,
planes of distance,

I thought of boutique dressing rooms brimming
with clothes and tension, like gas, expanding. And of two little girls
watching their mother cry at her reflection distorted in a fluorescent mirror.

The weight of her past made flesh on her hips,
the scars of our arrivals barely healed after all this time,
my blind hands all over the body.

Grasping, desperate to hold onto something real,
not knowing what that was.

(M)EAT

I sucked marrow from bones at dinner,
my father's face a bloody grin of pride. I ate liver in chunks
for breakfast, pink and firm, jewels to adorn my insides.
I gloried in the feel of flesh, the exertion of the chew.
Holding my mother's hand in the English Market,
I saw them – turkey chandeliers, plucked,
bruised purple eyelids dainty lightbulbs.
Their smell, fresh as the insides of my mouth.
Mother stroked my hair. *There, there*. I refused to eat
meat, became pillowy, meek. She hid muscle under mashed potato,
I tasted its tang in soup. *Eat up*, my parents said. I could not
swallow. My skin goose-pimple yellow, doctors drew blood
in tiny, regular sips. Teeth turned to glass and shattered
in my mouth. All I could taste was blood.

BIG GIRL

In the nightclub   I drank
Peach Schnapps   with ice
my heart   a nest of eggs
I wanted   all of you
to see   my tender belly
and not be   ashamed
I showed   only peacock eyes
my big   fuchsia   mouth

I wanted   to fill up
with the floppy compliance   of beautiful   wet tongues
flashing   in and out
under lights   Outside
after   kissing some   of you
or trying to   ample
for all   of you
I sucked chips   salty and bitter
gathered those   who remained
starving   too drunk to walk
home   into a circle
Around   I went   parting
lips   pushing masticated potato
onto the dent   of your   plump tongues
My saliva   in your stomachs
(stirring)
My pulse in   your necks
(hatching)

RESEARCHING THE IRISH FAMINE

*

Bulldozers disturb the old workhouse site,
uncover babies' skulls
curved like tiny moons. Their mothers
beside them, lullabies
locked in their jaws.

*

They can measure hunger now. Test
how much bellies rumbled, the stress
teeth were under, rotten
before they broke
scurvied gums.

*

Mothers exhausted their own bodies
to produce milk. High nitrogen
evidence of body tissue
breaking down,
recycling.

*

The starving
human
literally
consumes
itself.

*

Babies died
anyway. They all died. Wasted away
like potatoes
in the ground. The whole
country rotten.

*

What was left buried in memorial gardens,
alongside statues to honour hunger:
children with milky fat
teeth in braces.
All we do now is eat.

COUNT UGOLINO
OR HISTORY'S VAGUEST CANNIBAL

Ugolino, locked up
with your children in that tower,

dreaming you were all wolves
hunted and torn to pieces, gnawing

at your fingers in grief or hunger.
The only sound that of doors

being nailed shut. What did you do
when they begged you to eat them?

When they cried out, *Stop our suffering.*
You brought us into being dressed in this sad flesh,

now strip it all away. Their scrawny limbs reaching
towards you, heads limp with exhaustion,

a lack of light. Four dead children,
you so blind by the sixth day you spoke

to them as though they were alive. Hunger,
you say, proved stronger than grief.

INTERCESSION TO ST ANTHONY

I am on my knees.
Find him –

Was that his bald head bobbing,
a candle-flame on my horizon –
the scar a tell, upside-down horse shoe
with all the luck spilled out.

The earth is eating
my family up –
it practises sucking at the soles
of my shoes. I can't resist pressing

my fingers into its soil, smearing muck
on my face, war paint. But I'm a loser,
my father died when I wasn't looking.
Careless, I've mislaid

my keys again. I buzz around
a stupid bluebottle bouncing off
walls, where are they?
Where is he? I hit my head on a shelf.

I swear I have left my body –
then you let me see, St. Anthony,
I'm broke from you and now
a gift given back –

a missing leopard print sock,
the lost gold earring,
my keys and now –
his clear white bones

licked clean, burning the ground.
I get up; the scar dissolved, the candle quenched,

there. There he is –

MOBY-DICK

I never imagined that
in Arrowhead when I encouraged you to purchase
a set of engravings of the whale and Ahab that
they would end up six years later
in your airy Dublin apartment,

the one that you share with your Canadian girlfriend.

'Look,' you say when I visit
for the first time,
'we hung the whale above the fireplace.'
You have left the bedroom door open and I see
the other picture hangs easily over your white bed.

Life, perverse origami, folds and twists and shapes itself
so that in your apartment, my coat lies on your crisp sheets.
I watch it from the living room,
beached upon that ivory shore,
as I sip weak tea.

ON THE PUBLICATION OF *LES TERRES DU CIEL* (1884)

Dearest Camille,

I want you; I want you to take skin
from my back, my shoulders,
skin that covers my breasts.

The highwayman James Allen
covered a memoir with his hide, a gift
to a brave man he tried to rob.

The judicial proceedings of murderer
John Horwood are sandwiched
in his largest organ.

Anatomy texts are bound
with skin of dissected cadavers,
de Sade's *Justine et Juliette* has nipples.

I want to cradle *Les Terres du Ciel*
between my thighs, my soul
passing from planet to planet. To be

a citizen of the sky, cross its universe faster
than light, touch that jagged lunar crescent,
see Saturn glowing scarlet and sapphire.

You think me frivolous, a society woman.
You are wrong. I know constellations will reign
in noise before existence, stars burn after our sun

dies. I want a world covered with telescopes.
Earth is only a chapter, less than that, a phrase,
less still, a word. Let me carry it.

HUNGER STRIKES (BROKEN SEQUENCE)

1. Hunger Strikes Catherine of Siena (1347–1380)

My sister taught me how.
Oh Bonaventura, they wanted
me to marry him, the slack-jawed widower.

I vomited twigs, hid in the convent,
wore a widow's habit. The other nuns complained
until at twenty-one I met Him.

He presented me with a ring fashioned from His skin.
Told me this sliver of flesh bound us,
wait, He told me, promising it would be special.

I levitated; only ate His body, others did not
understand how good it was
to kiss His holy prepuce.

Oh, Bonaventura, I am a house of sticks,
my bones rattle with desire until I lick it.
I feel it quiver, alive on my tongue.

2. Hunger Strikes Angela of Foligno (1248–1309)

I drink pus from wounds of the unclean.
Christ, it is like water to me, sweet
as the Eucharist.
                I pick
                at their scabs, chew them flat
                between my teeth.
The lice I pluck and let drown
on my tongue sustain me.
Lord, I am the Host.
                Lead me in the light
                to the summit of perfection.
                I will pray and pray
and pray to you: to remain poor,
be obedient, chaste and humble.
This is all I ask. God-man, feed me.

3. Hunger Strikes Veronica Giuliani (1660–1727)

My confessor ordered her to do it,
the novice kicked me again and again.

Her shoe pummelled my teeth,
bloodied my lips. I did not stir
or whimper, I kept my mouth open.

I remained bruised for weeks.

When my face was almost pink again
He prompted me to clean the walls and floor

of my cell with my tongue. I licked
for hours, scraping up each wisp of skin and hair.
My throat became thick with cobwebs,

my mind clear as light.

4. Hunger Strikes Columba of Rieti (1467–1501)

My body is a temple I keep
clean for You, spotless –
lashing my skin so it grows

tired of bleeding.
Wearing hair shirts I cannot forget
what it means to be alert.

I have toured the Holy Land in visions.
I don't imagine they would understand
what I see.

When they came for me, the men,
they ripped off my robes
expecting to find me virginal,

untouched.
How they gasped in horror!
How glad I was that I had used myself

like an old rag.
Beating myself with that spiked
chain shielded me,

my breasts and hips so deformed
they ran from me,
screaming.

5. *Hunger Strikes Gemma Galgani (1878–1903)*

Chapter 1: St. Gemma's Birth and Early Education: First Flowers of
Virtue. Her Mother's Death

Chapter 2: St. Gemma's life at Home. Her Heroic Patience in Great
Trials

Chapter 3: St. Gemma's Dangerous Illness and Miraculous Recovery

Chapter 4: St. Gemma Tries to Enter Religion. She is Not Received

Chapter 5: St. Gemma Receives the Stigmata

Chapter 6: St. Gemma Meets the Passionist Fathers. More About the
Stigmata

Chapter 7: St. Gemma's Characteristic Virtue

Chapter 8: The Means by Which St. Gemma Attained Perfection.
First, her Detachment

Chapter 9: St. Gemma's Perfect Obedience

Chapter 10: St. Gemma's Profound Humility

Chapter 11: St. Gemma's Heroic Mortification

Chapter 12: Attacks by the Devil[1]

Chapter 13: St. Gemma's Gift is Raised on the Wings of
Contemplation to the Highest Degree of Divine
Love[2]

Chapter 14: St. Gemma's Last Sickness[3]

Chapter 15: St. Gemma's Death and Burial[4]

---

1   All night I dream of food, Jesus take my taste from me. Rip out my
tongue and I will expiate, through my bleeding for you, all the sins
committed by your shrouded men.
2   For sixty days I vomited whenever I ate.
3   I was tormented by banquets.
4   Am I threatened by flesh or its opposite?

HUNGER STRIKES VICTORIA KENNEFICK

She punches her stomach loose, blind-
naked like a baby mole.
In the shower she cannot wash herself clean
the way she'd like. Rid herself
of useless molecules. Would that she
could strip her bones,
be something
neat,
complete.
Useful.

To eat or not to eat,
switch table sides.
Stuff cheese sandwiches
and chocolate blocks into a wide
moist orifice. Or, alternatively
zip that mouth
closed like a jacket,
a body already
contained within.
It doesn't need
to feed.

But I have set a table for us all.
For us all, a feast!
On a vast, smooth cloth, already soiled.
Let's take a seat, eat our fill.
You know you want to,
dig in.

NIGHTBABY

I've never thought about the moon so much,
considered it sister-like, watching us learn
how to be together. You in my arms, perfect
circle of your small mouth pressed to my breast.
Lunar light from my phone, my own brain, the moon
all shining. It's scary how big the night is, how small
we are in it. Think of the others up with us,
a night-nation of milk and mouths, all fumbling
towards each other in the dark, singing.
The shape of you, a crescent against me. Little planet
exploring your phases. Oh, moon be good to her
in the ebb-and-flow of monthly life. Lick the path clean.
But for now sweet Nightbaby, rock with me.

*

VICTORIA KENNEFICK is a poet, writer and teacher from Shanagarry, Co. Cork now based in Co. Kerry. She holds a doctorate in English from University College Cork and studied at Emory University and Georgia College and State University as part of a Fulbright Scholarship. Her research on the short stories of Flannery O'Connor and Frank O'Connor was also funded by an IRCHSS Scholarship and a MARBL Fellowship. Her pamphlet, *White Whale* (Southword Editions, 2015), won the Munster Literature Centre Fool for Poetry Chapbook Competition and the Saboteur Award for Best Poetry Pamphlet. Her work has appeared in *Poetry*, *The Poetry Review*, *Poetry Ireland Review*, *The Stinging Fly*, *Poetry News*, *Prelude*, *Copper Nickel*, *The Irish Times*, *Ambit*, *bath magg*, *Banshee*, *Southword*, *Bare Fiction* and elsewhere. She won the 2013 Red Line Book Festival Poetry Prize and many of her poems have also been anthologised and broadcast on national radio stations. A recipient of a Next Generation Artist Award from the Arts Council of Ireland, she has received bursaries from Kerry County Council and Words Ireland. She was a co-host of the Unlaunched Books Podcast and is on the committee of Listowel Writers' Week, Ireland's longest-running literary festival. Her first book is due from Carcanet in 2021.

Acknowledgements –
The Poetry Review
The Stinging Fly
Still in the Dreaming Anthology
Ambit
Bare Fiction
Southword
Poetry Day Ireland Poem 2020

Farsi is the second tongue that in part guides the poems' visions and makes them want to blush. It's such a rich and astonishing language, and I have such poor command of it. Yet this linguistic deficiency also draws some of the more pure, literal meanings and images from the syntax and the sayings. The sounds are not impressed upon with meaning initially, for me. So I return in Farsi like a child in the language, with the visceral gaze, and no shame for that. I offer 'translations', reluctantly.

A poem begins with a colour, an image, the beat of a line that might bruise itself into my mind, sometimes for long periods. That becomes ritual, the rhythm is repeated or the thing chants itself visually across the eye, sometimes a note or set of dashes or scribbles, revisited. Eventually, those foci begin to soften; the colours may seep out into a wider palette, the image catches its story, language falls into the line. This happens at the point of writing, and meaning arrives sonically, intuitively. These are the better poems.

Often, I'll try to capture the essence of that arrival by remaining true to the image clarified, in a microcosmic way. I want to write about many things, but in the poems that I begin with clear intention for meaning, some message, or sharpened point, these do not work well.

I think of what Mina Loy says about 'Poetry [as] prose bewitched, a music made of visual thoughts, the sound of an idea', and that resonates with me.

For the *thing* to stand for itself then is enough, and I have learnt, or am still learning, that it does not need to carry the weight of every*thing*, to hold its voice in the world. Transformative as the process can be, these poems try to hold fast to looking at, and for, the universe within the bluebottle, or in an apartment in Tehran.

The cast of characters being called up are not asked then, to speak for more than the moment and form they inhabit. Or, at least, I have tried to avoid imposing on them that responsibility. I read them as caught between glass well slides; a tiny drop, magnified, and slipped between pages, big and full enough, in and of themselves. To speak of the pomegranate's fall from Saveh, the milk jar, or Abdul's pouring of rice, is just that.

In many of these poems, the visceral gaze comes from the child's mind, returned to through the figure of Gabriel and his noticings. Poets are awful thieves, and I am indebted, indeed guilty, of crimes against his fresh eyes and sparkling imagination. But there is licence, and also bribery, in the poems' gifts of a blackbird, or party horns.

I like it when sound and colour pull through forms, how they swell a sonnet or pull it close. This is perhaps the firmest restraint I apply to poems. Sometimes it doesn't work, and *free* verse overcomes the form, but for others, the form submits and that can be a useful source of discipline, generate meaning of its own. I also enjoy the game.

*

ALL BLUE THINGS

I was once a chicken heart;
small, singing down the river

I was once a standing bear; twi
-light claws; rainbow salmon scales

I was once an aging man;
sat, watching them deliver

our whole universe;
dark, backed into the soil

And one time when an old skin
had rotted blue on me, I was

a snake,
a night-time birch,

an elderly mother
of three sunk girls.

They were pink skin
and purple-seahorse curls

I was once the mastodon
in children's crayon scrawls

Once the liver leaking bubble
on the knife and board,

or the feather fallen
onto Morecambe Bay

MANGO BRUISE
(a sonnet)

Inside my right thigh
there is a Neptune bruise
turning to
red moon and

Sparse constellations
in the pores,
drying blood
clotting stars

And a sweet hurt
every time
I send a finger
into space

This mango bruise   each day   gets more
and more   sunny at the heart

POPPY BRUISE

It came
as someone else's poppy bruise, but
now has blued into a sort of
Neptune on my inner thigh
battle wound
starship badge for
showing off
for falling off the bike, now

Fading   slow
into dispersing constellations of
dry   blood in pores:
clotting stars

Sometimes, I like to reach a finger out
and press into the sky

ABDUL

Seventeen sacks
of rice grain came
pouring on his toes   he'd
stabbed each pack stacked
on the shelves that lined a wall along
the back part of his father's shop: Patel's

angry   at the lies people can tell
                    all about him   were
                        mad clouds   of
Paki of *Camel-Carter* of *Dirty*
Arab of *Terrorist*
Cell of
            Radicalization
            all
floating round his face
and beard

but now:
the cool slide
        of off-white rice
                    falling

          down his
      open ankles;
Rolling
 down the skin on
      phalanges in-between
      his toes and
      filling   up towards these clouds,
felt
   like dry ablution.

Struck here   to this hard ground he
curled his toes through
      these
       bits of heaven rising,
   cold silk up his shins,

he could stand here for a long time
      and speak
             think
  only ever
     pearl rice.

SEPIDEH

There is a small village near Shiraz, cracking
by the mountains' foot, pinning down

earth. There is a girl, she has letters
which she speaks to Einstein through,

translated into stars. She has been banned
from standing in the mountain's palm at night

by her mahram, who has no or little time. She
has married a man with a PhD

so she can fly far, to the US, to study
constellations. Anousheh invited her. *Dige.*

* *dige / another*

SHADE
(the mullah)

There is a *sofreh*, in a small apartment in Tehran, there is *chai* sweetened
with *nabat* a taxi man talking to Azita, Koroush, Behnam:

 'I told him!,   "get out / *boro biroon*
tuye aftab beshin   un derakht moleh shoma niste   in riye

-ye Iran." by God   it's what I did!' He swirls the *nabat* round. 'Picked
him up off Khoddami St. standing in the shade of that *chenar*

and drove him up a few feet before I stopped the car, said
"get out!" he said *"agha   chikar-mikoni to?"*

"I picked you up   because you were stood under our tree
I want you to stand under the heat of the sun - now wait."' *Dige.*

* *dige / another*

ABSENCE (*OF THE BIRDS*)

on a jammed road in some far-off eastern land; a bulbul seller, in pink,
masked, beige cap. There is a man, approached by the seller crouched

at the silver Range Rover driver side, who reaches out. The seller reaches in
to the hexagon cage, and bird
        by
             bird balances the exchange of feather and toman.

Each time he puts a nightingale into the buyer's hand extending
from the rolled-down window, the palm opens, each truth-song

flight, while Emilee Flood and Lofi sing
'if it's quite alright'. They say

on Twitter that *not all heroes wear capes*. They also
say, *this is custom: buy a bird, release, pray*. And the poacher,
                keeps on. *Dige*

             * *dige / another*

THE AVOCADO TREE

When I come to you, tall glass/ *ikea*
plastic cup/ milk jar in hand and pour
for you; life. When I don't come soon
enough, watch your flopping leaves
knowing your soil is dry, the conversation
in me can go on. But in time

I rise and take the ten steps
to the kitchen sink, pulling muscles;
calves, glutes, thighs, through such
sorrow, on the brink of water-eyes.
Knowing too well   this desire for entering
the natural world. By sheer fluke

or accidental swirl into humanity
I find myself, bending, by this avocado
tree; grown from pip in *Gü* jar
on toothpicks and still water; Gabriel
and me. Look over

its green and reddened crown
of fronds beaming, so skinny
going down, into the terracotta
deepening, assure myself that I am all
-owed compassion
for why else

would I water
    water the voiceless

THE PARSLEY POT

and the fern, curling at the tips.
The bluebottle landing, looping
green metallic glass, matt wing,
how life comes out of it

as big as mine; an eclipse
of our bodies as we sit, watching
Elizabeth's rose, bobbing its heavy
head as the breeze blows

yellow. We are basking in the sun,
small and mellow, thinking of *sharia*;
and the *fiqh* of forty lashes, for cruelty
to life

SWIMMING

It's so obvious to walk into sea
WATER to feel alive because the cold
FILLS around the bottom of your
BODY and it's so obvious to walk
OUT when the cold has adjusted and you
can't feel it anymore to feel ALIVE
  and HEAVIER and DRIPPING and
it's so obvious to hope the sun is out
so that you can walk and APPRECIATE
DRYING in the SUN or to hope for
HAIL and COLD that makes you
JUST COLDER while you tread and
tremble home. It's so obvious for a woman
to do this

THE ESTATE
(Arrowfield)

     Way of entries   lamp light gloom
on the whistle that calls at night.
Package in the hedgerow; hawthorn blossom rushing on
ancestral spite; hooded angels transacting veinal-escalation
for metal cuts, paper slights   They adorn their wings
with these. Uncollected bins   that night creepers fill
with used nappies, fast penknives. The playground is colourful fists and
council brews help call out each child's name *gone
walkabout.* Grey slabs sleeted   with balloon canisters, and Gabriel

asks about these; *bullet shells / silver beans.* So in our garden,
some way to the back, we have planted *things* and given to them names
of the highest order, of which   Parivash is fairy queen; fourteen
foot shade, candle that sears a slot in our sky and gleans the unseen there,
    also
angels need a way to fare better; flowers   for the late spring; cream cups

ta'ârofing Behzād's filigree in cinnabar, gold beanstalk curving down to
    reach
      magnolia grandiflora – evergreen
                    And these,
                      high gloss leaves
                            that point to

* *Parivash, meaning 'fairy queen' in Farsi*

* *ta'ârof, to engage in the Iranian art of etiquette and civility, a verbal duel,
a waltz of words*

* *Kamāl ud-Dīn Behzād, Persian painter and miniaturist (c. 1450 – 1535)*

FROG,

on the living room rug! at 8:55 just before
setting off for *Forest Club*. The thick whittling

stick in the yellow bag slung
nearby. Frog on the rug, at five to nine,

fawn-brown legs, camo-chest, wheatish arms,
green rimmed eyes, then the fuchsia tongue!

party horn curling slowly up
& down in a young boy's
mouth, not just pretending
to be

                amphibian!

STARLING

      we had said goodbye
              for the first part of the night
and I   stood by your bed, while
you asked me   *why should we love God*
(– *the mostest* – you had later clarified
      you meant)

            ~~I had just come home from sliding on a path~~
      ~~the curb that caught the front wheel of the Cannondale~~
         ~~and concrete that   had scraped off half my palms~~
    ~~left   paper-skin on the ground near Princess Road~~
      ~~on the way back from Didsbury Mosque. (they do~~
~~circles on a Wednesday~~

              ~~to teach the basics of~~ *~~deen~~*~~)~~

       sitting   with my palms upturned
and stinging   round some red and yellow
islands bubbling raw

I have learnt   that maybe
I am preaching
what I do not know

Gabriel,
     I put your questions on a black bird
     and sent them to the sky

JIGARREH-MAN
(which you said you'd eat)

       plapped here on the tabletop
for just under one week and rotting, blood and sour. Is this

the *nastaran* you threw me to the stars
in. is this the way to say goodbye

  where we are from? i've been
  watching   your last seen date and time *jigarr*

jiggar on crushing petals in my lungs squeezing
the last drops of oil into these ducts that are liars.

So my pain is pink, and that record
fingered out on the chopping board; white,

around my liver which you said
that you would eat

*jigarreh-man, literally meaning 'my liver', though typically used
as a term of love and endearment
*jigar / liver
*nastaran / wild rose

RED CITIES

I came to this planet earth
with cherries hanging on my ears

and I was not a girl.
I am also that girl.

I followed the path of the horse's gallop,
by a setar that played without strings

and I was not a musician. I am
also that hand that plays. The man

dropped a coin for my sound.
I am that man. The glint rolled as sound

loaded a horn so loud it banged
and worth was fashioned   well. I am

a bursted eardrum. The ear felt
wind sigh past. Wind cuts across

the ear. That ear is me.
The ear is a house that rests

on water with stilts that wobble.
Those stilts are me. And that house

belongs to me. Mine is my name
and my body. The body is

me   where no maps are drawn.
The pencil belongs to me. I am

the belonger, and he is mine and me. Mine
is a home of cherry trees and they are

sharpened. I am the stone from one
eaten. That meal is me and I kneel

before the mouth that does.
Teeth are me. Gums.

The tongue is enough.
I am taste buds and they

flower an orchard every June.
I am June. My Mother is Joon.

Joon is a place over bitter seas.
I am that. I do not sail past blue lines.

* joon, meaning 'dear' in Farsi

ANOR ANOR

                  i was once a
pomegranate too   but people
kept pulling at my chunks for quarters
        that they'd made inside their two

eyes, looking at me
when I was first laid on the table
after cuttings from my tree, i was the rose
        of all fruit bowls,

picked by *zan Ali*. After that   his blade
was the one that sliced me in four parts
and enjoyed that break inside as he pulled
me open like a lily

        cleft to bloom. The toothpick
for each of my little gems.   The pink juice
dribbling on the plate and down his chin,
       i didn't mind that.

      How many times   if you knew
        i have thought of that
wet travel through his beard
       after *Saveh*, after

        dropping off
           that lower lip
now
      I am pink stained skin
     cream only

in the parts where he missed with slips of tongue

or spits from under fingertips
   and ruptures in   the pull-apart.
   Limp. And see

           how well my skin   leathers
as i   bloodmoon on the plate for him
waiting   for him to come back to
     my three left crescents

*

MARYAM HESSAVI is a British, Manchester-based poet and critic, with poems and reviews appearing in various magazines. An alumnus of the University of Manchester, she holds an MA in English Literature, with specialisms in Modernism, Creative Writing and Linguistics. Maryam is a Ledbury Critic, freelance writer and contributing editor at *Ambit Magazine*. She is also a committee member for the Manchester-based poetry reading series Poets and Players.

It was never a choice for me to write about my childhood and the people who have shaped my imagination – it was a rite of passage and an eagerness to remember. The small streets of Negril, Jamaica, where the sea is visible from all directions, the landscapes, with the great river winding through the morass and dividing the town into two halves – the wealthy and the working-class, are always there whenever I am thinking of a new poem to write. I write fictitiously and creatively about my experiences, the ones that have left the most striking impression on me. These impressions evolve in accordance with the poetics of storytelling – ones that give a life that is far more splendid or superficial than that of the life of the actual muse.

The majority of these poems are set in the vivid fishing village of 1980s Negril. Compositions such as 'The Crab-Catchers', 'Mischief', 'Michael', 'The Frog At Night', and 'Paper Kite' reflect communities who shared an 'interdependency.' The early eighties seems an innocuous decade when strangers could be trusted, funerals were conduits of tradition, as delineated in 'Nine-Night' and 'Paper Kite'. Back then, folklore was more than mere myth. Parents knew the streets were safe enough to allow their children to roam the morass and the sidewalks along the beach road in search of those mud-loving brachyura.

Negril had only a few hotels then, which were predominantly owned by local residents. Hippies were still sleeping in tents on the beach and knocking on doors, renting accommodation from benevolent matriarchs, ones akin to the old lady in 'The Swivel Chair', 'Michael' and 'Nine-Night'. These matriarchs were charitable homeowners who were willing to transform their homes into a B&B for the stranded local or the adventurous traveller, regardless of country, colour, or class.

Negril then was not like Negril today. Fishing and tourism were the two major economies. My uncle, who suffered from delusions, was a seine-pulling fisherman. He would leave his bed in the early hours in the morning and would walk nearly two miles to the sea. He would come home around midday with his catch of pink, blue, and yellow parrotfish and a pocket filled with money. Nearly all the men in Negril, who were born before the Independence, were fishermen. Many had followed their fathers and uncles into the backbreaking trade. The poem 'Howard's Oars' tries to capture my uncle's schizophrenia while seeking to emulsify his condition with his vocation. Looking back now, it was those moments of madness that were his most defining features.

Towards the beginning of the millennium, HIV Aids was becoming widespread in Negril. More people were rumoured to have died from the disease, and deaths that were attributed to cancer were said to be HIV-related. Moreover, people were accused of deliberately infecting others with the disease. During that time of despair, churches were filled with those who were anxious about their immortal souls. 'Go Tell The Mountains' and 'The Tadpoles' Pond' try to shine a light on this frightful period in Negril's history.

Many had left Negril in search of a better life. Some were successful in their pursuits while others were less fortunate, as is portrayed in 'The Swivel Chair', 'If Me Did Know' and 'Winston'. In these lived experiences, the poetic voice is never still. Each poem is an unravelling of memories, which are adapted to fit the poetic conventions.

*

PAPER KITE

When you are a child, you think you will
never die, not until you see someone like you
lying in a small white casket
and you are standing there next to a mother,
watching her cry, thinking that if a child
aged eight could die, then so could I.

A small crowd had gathered on wet soil,
with the sun going down behind the locust tree.
The singing grew as Lamar's casket was lowered
into a half-hole. A girl, aged five was thrown
across the grave three times. Her father was afraid
that she too might die if Lamar's ghost

could not learn to forget his past and the living.
I too wanted to be thrown across the grave, but no
one thought it was necessary or perhaps they knew
Lamar did not need me as much as I thought he did.
The crowd stayed until the casket was sealed in
before leaving him to rest

with the older dead. I walked in between the rows
of guinep trees, hoping that if I was to go
to the shops that night, that I would not smell the fresh
ointment on his skin or see him crossing the lane back
to his mother, back to his little room where the tail
of his paper kite still flutters in the wind.

MISCHIEF

I'm not going to tell you who poisoned the old
Tamarind tree. I'm not ready to disclose who was swinging from the
branch or what happened before they landed.
I'm not going to tell you about the empty fishing boat,
sinking. I'm not ready to tell you what happened to the shark that pulled
it in. I'm not going to tell you who tied the plastic around the shark's
    head,
or who started the fire under granny's bed.
I'm not ready to tell you who smoked the last cigarette, the tobacco,
and the seaweed from the cabinet. I'm not going to tell you who stole the
    money
from the letter, the mattress, and the saving can.
I'm not going to tell you who drank the Appleton rum,
then hid the bottle under the drum.
I'm not ready to disclose who muddied the white blankets on the wire,
drying. I'm not going to tell you who wore your favorite slipper,
or whose dog chewed up the leather strap.
I'm not going to tell you who set fire to the cat's tail
or who puts it out with a blanket from the trunk.
I'm not readying to disclose who ate both
jonnie-cakes and the four chicken legs,
for uncle Sam's dinner.
I'm not going to tell you how I know all this.
don't ask me to squeal who done it!
No, I can't tell you about the match-sticks, the toxin
or the rope on the old fruit tree.
I can't tell you whose boat it was
or where the shark ended up.
I can't tell you about the rum, the weed
or who mixed in the mud.
I'm not going to tell you where I saw your English money,
spending. It wasn't your dog that bites through your slipper,

and I'm not going to tell you whose it was
because if I did, then it wouldn't be mischief.

THE SWIVEL CHAIR

The old lady had once had a daughter that died
in New York. Her body was shipped home and buried
under a jackfruit tree. Her apartment stripped
and a swivel chair sent across the Caribbean Sea.
The chair arrived on a Friday in a large brown box.
The old lady loved the chair because it showed
the life her daughter had. She placed the chair
on the verandah next to her wicker bench.
All summer the chair on its metal column
turned and turned and turned. The old lady feared
that the chair would cease to be
a swivel chair if the turning did not stop.
In the heat of the sun, the chair turned and turned
and turned. Its molasses-coloured oil seeped up
from its base as the chair turned and turned.
The neighbours who came to the old lady's house
watched the chair turn right round, then left, and right
round again. The old lady was kind and the local children
enjoyed sitting on her verandah eating mangoes
and singing ring-game songs.
The children also liked spinning on the foreign chair:
never had they seen a chair that goes round and round
like a merry-go-round. The old lady knew that the chair
would not last if the turning did not stop and would
ask the children not to spin as much. But the children would
not listen. Each day they'd come to the old lady's verandah
and whirl and whirl on the swivel chair, laughing, whooping,

and singing. They did not know what the chair meant.
The old lady did not tell them that the chair had belonged to
her only daughter. Instead, she would ask them
not to spin as much, but the swivel chair turned
and turned until one day
the old lady's soft voice faltered. She did not ask the children
to stop as she had done before. She watched them turn
and turn the memory of her child into creaks and oil.
And each day the children came and sat down
in pairs singing: dirty bus, dirty bus, round and round,
donkey want water, wash him down.
As the sun was setting behind the sea,
the chair began to squeak and squeak, as if
the voice of her dead daughter was calling from within
the leather seat. The children heard the squeak
but kept on spinning and spinning and spinning.
The old lady watched in silence as the metal column
grew longer and longer. It rose up until she could see its
metal tip sharp. The seat tumbled to the floor.
The children were still clinging on when it crashed
to the ground. They squealed and laughed,
and giggled. The children tried to push the column back
inside the base but could not. They drifted off,
leaving the chair in halves. The old lady watched the children go
one by one. She looked at the broken chair and thought
of her daughter's voice and the children's song
and felt something swells inside her heart. She called her son
to take the base and the seat to the back room and lock them in
with the bed-foot and frame of her daughter's things.
Whenever the old lady passed by the door she could hear
the children's song haunting the room. At night when she could
not sleep, she would hear her daughter's voice singing
in a foreign accent: dirty bus, dirty bus, round and round,
donkey wants water, wash him down.

IF ME DID KNOW

I didn't know what possessed me
to take the seat of a stranger.

I was on a plane from Montego Bay
when a woman asked

me to exchange seats. I am a good
Jamaican, so I did.

when the plane stopped in London
a man in white shirt

with a pen in him pocket escort me
through a back gate.

'You didn't eat your meal', him say.
'So you must be a drug

mule!' A drug-mule? Is what him say
to me? I am a forty-nine

year old woman from the gully. The
only mule I know was

Maas Allen's old donkey, who had one
good foot and a chewed

off ear. Him showed me to a doctor's
bed and told me to let down

me hair. To take off me clothes,
to show me-self like pickney

chasing fresh air. When me holler 'After
me no done noting!'

him left him chair and came back with a
woman. 'Is your name

Wendy Martin?' I told them it wasn't.
She opened my passbook,

saw Tanya Weir. 'You're saying you're
not Martin?' 'Is that me say

is hear you can't hear?' We went on
like this till the tea them

bring was a cup of ice. And me start
to forget why me board

the blue and white bird in the first
place. The woman gave

me back me clothes and told me to
enjoy my stay. I could

a cut me eyes on her, but I couldn't
wait. I saw me brother standing

far away, him mobile phone to him ear.
Him waved, came running over.

I couldn't look him in the face or tell
him why me was so so late.

THE TADPOLES' POND

for Georgette

With a quart bottle of oil,
a rolled tissue for a wick,
you walk through the field,
shading the flame from the breeze.

You can hear the preacher's voice
over the hill, calling all
sinners to come to the pond
where the tadpoles swim.

From the top of the hill, you
see a long white tent, sparkling,
and hear the preacher singing:
all wrong doers come,

come on down to the pond where
the tadpoles swim and forsake
the old you, your old ways, till
your burdens grow light.

You blow out the lesser lamp
and run to the bigger glow,
till you reach the tent. Sinners
kneeling on their knees.

The preacher rests his hand on
your pendent head and tells you
to be free of all evil.
Free your mind and heart

from all principalities.
You wait at the side and watch
the saints speaking in new tongues,
jerking and ticking.

One comes to you carrying
a tadpole in a clear jar.
She whispers, *what would you gain*
if Christ comes tonight

and you are here left behind?
She gives you the jar and tells
you to follow the sinners,
down into the pond.

But you are scared now holding
your jar, watching your tadpole
swim, observing the sinners
getting in the pond

and wading up to their waist.
They freed their tadpoles, their tails
fanning next to legs kicking
back into the past.

They are creating a new
them. But you know that you could
never return to that life
to be born again.

You turn to leave as the new
saints crawl from the lake
into a new life, but you will hide
and feed your tadpole.

THE CRAB-CATCHERS

Popping torchlight brought
the children and their rippling shadows
to the morass where the bush-crabs
rested at the mangrove's edge:

Crabs up to their bellies in mud,
seated by their doors. With giant claws
pillowed on sludge, their dotted eyes
watched shadows passing before the moon.

Each child, armed with crocus-bags
and bottles of light, looked like fireflies
caught in the thickets in the night,
with mosquitos playing Jonkonnu on fifes.

The crabs, seeing the darkness exploding
with light, turned away from the moon.
They scrambled on their stiletto legs
and dashed down their watery holes.

Stretching and reaching
through the escapees' doors, with optic hands
the children brought the crabs back
to face the knots in the burlap bags.

Now tip-toeing on their neighbours' carapaces,
they foam and watch the sky from the bottom
of a drum, waiting for a cloud to stand still
before the mongoose sun.

MICHAEL

He came when the sun was still setting.
His long fingers gripping the steering
of his wooden handcart as its four rubber
wheels crept over the hill. He had brought
with him his jerk chicken drum and an empty

bag with room for leaving. His large bloodshot
eyes were kind, so when he offered to pay
our grandmother for a night's bed,
he left his cart and drum by the front door
and marched across the hall to the spare room.

When daylight came, we found a pudding
pan stacked with chicken foot and gizzards
sunning on the lawn. He must have spent the night
cleaning the birds he had brought tucked in his cart
with his ten-inch knife.

Around midday, his hands were red with spice
from rubbing paprika into the meat.
He unpacked the coals and arranged the meat
on the grill. At dusk, he pushed his cart back down
the hill. We didn't think we would see him again.

At half-past three, in the early hours, he had returned
knocking on the windows. Our grandmother opened
the door. He came in looking disappointed.
His chicken was still in the drum and he had used
up all his money on supplies.

She showed him back to the spare room and told him,
'People in Negril only eat from those

they know. But with time, everyone will know who you
is.' That morning, he fed us the meat with fried rice for
breakfast, then for lunch, and told us he was considering
pimping.

WINSTON

Winston
you know, it wasn't rude
you asking to move to Manchester
where you pictured the streets ripe with gold.

You sitting on dada's bed
fear quivering up your lips
waiting to hear the words
he'll live…, you didn't.

His dreadlocks spread out like a black
cotton sheet spoiled by the stillness
of his wide eyes. Can you remember saying,
'I should a burned his thin body down to the bones'?

You sighing a breath of relief
when I said, 'the police would get you'.
Ms Sylvia coming close
telling me, 'Here is your father!'

I looked at you sitting on the rock,
your voice like dad's
'Here is your father!'
It stayed with me for a long time.

Winston
I must tell you, England
is hard, nothing worth having is free.
No grave mourners or coconut trees.

No nesberry, star-apple, or sweet-sop,
nor yellow-tail fish boiling with
scotch-bonnet in a dutch-pot.
You would hate the beach-less streets

curse at the biting east wind and swear at the slow lazy
rain. You would despise daytime TV,
bin your bangers and mash
and pour a pound of salt on the toad in the hole.

Winston
I must tell you; it wasn't rude of you to ask.

HOWARD'S OARS

He was ruled by the full grey moon
the fourth son of Maroon and German blood.
Eyes deep blue, his hands inured
to pulling daily seines to canoes,
until noon.

He was divided by a malignant star
the only child to be born of the lunar touch.
Once a year he would vanish into the coral
wilderness of his spurious mind,
and its swelling scar.

He would lay siege in the oarless zinc kitchen –
in his barracuda's den, where he scaled his nephew's
flesh with his swordfish's blade. Like a noxious
eel drowned by a kerosene fire,
his mind was let back in.

He would have no memory of the day before
and would sit beneath his yellow door and tell
the story of a giant fish with stings and wings
and moonshine eyes, which stole
his oars and watched him die.

NINE-NIGHT

Ena had laid out her black dress and stockings
on the bed to let the creases un-crease
and selected her fan for the service in the Anglican
Church.

The Wake singers were scratching on their graters,
playing pot-cover-lids, and beating their drums
while the crowd danced and sang:
Roll Jordan Roll.

Her daughter's body had been brought home from Canada
by her four children. It was the night before the
funeral. Ena sat on the verandah gazing
at the festivity,

aware that Dalton, her eldest son had taken his sister's death
to heart and was laid up in bed breathing heavily.
She knocked the ashes from her billiard pipe
and listened, with her hands

on her lap, to the hired voices singing. Come tomorrow
she knew their songs would turn hers to tears. Ena
saw the darkened sky above the crowd
flash with streaks of lightning.

The mento band stopped beating. A cloud of smoke
from a brick fire drifted over the crowd.
She saw men running towards the back of the house
carrying buckets filled with melted ice.

The drum cooking the curry-goat was on fire.
Ralston had got up to use the bathroom,
when the smoke floated through the glass panes
and fogged the room.

Ena's youngest son came and stood in the doorway
looking down at her in her wicker chair. His breath
fumed with overproof when he said, *'You not going
to look at you son, the fucker's in there dying?'*

She got up without rebuking him and hurried
to the back room. Ralston was placed on her bed,
face cotton coloured. He was laid out next to the dress
she would wear in the morning, then nine days after.

Ena took a bucket of water and bathed his feet.
She ordered the band to play but the storm
had begun to descend. They waited as the rain
and thunder bellowed on the zinc roof.

GO TELL THE MOUNTAINS

Go tell it to the tall man who didn't care
none about your health, Novelette.

Go tell it to the young men who will care
and fear the killer in you, Georgette

Go tell it to the Anglican priest, he cares
if your soul burns in hell, Novelette.

Go tell it to Jesus, see if He truly cares
about the sores on your legs, Novelette.

Go cry it to the doctor, he should care
more about your sex life, Novelette.

Go break it to your granny, she will care
about the shame it brings, Novelette.

Go tell it to your mother, she clearly cares
more about her rum bottle, Novelette.

Go spill it to your son, he shows he cares
about the days you have left, Novelette.

Go tell the mountains your fears and cares
go tell the mountains, Novelette.

THE FROG AT NIGHT

Sitting on a powdery ground slowly
soaking out the green banana stains,
a metal tub is filled with clothes up to its brim.

The force of each hand squeezes the suds
over the edge spilling the smell of blue soap
and Clorox bleach, as each

garment is submerged below the surface
of milky water, changed by cubes
of Reckitt's Crown Blue.

Then came the sound of washing:
'scrups, scrups'. The non-flexible
whites were left overnight to soften up.

Steadily beneath the moonlight
under the banana trees, the water
stagnated until a speckled frog leaping

past plopped in by curiosity and sat still
on the raft of clothes like on lily-pods
until its lycra began to strip

clean from its freckled body. As the cloud
shadowed the moonlight it hopped off
into the fields trying to shake the heat

of the tub. In the morning, its thin pigments
floated above the clothes, colouring
each garment with spotted fragments.

*

CHRISTINE ROSEETA WALKER was born in Jamaica and lives in the United Kingdom. She began writing poetry and fiction whilst studying for her first degree at the University of Salford. In 2018, she enrolled on the MA in Creative Writing at the University of Manchester where her love for writing poetry flourished. She graduated with Distinction and was published that year with *bath magg* poetry magazine. The following year, her work appeared in *PN Review* and *Wild Court*. She visits Negril, Jamaica at least once a year but lives in the Cheshire countryside, from where she writes and coaches Creative Writing and Poetry Writing, virtually, to a group of students in the UAE.

These poems move from Northern Germany to the battlefields of Flanders and the Somme, from Poenari Castle, Romania – one of Vlad the Impaler's homes – to Penang, Malaysia – a crucial entrepôt for British ships on their way to China loaded with opium. They take in a raging Boudica, a pathetic King Arthur, several versions of Dracula, a mournful Romanian spook in exile and a range of mouldy Victorians. In every line they are – as David Scott puts it to Stuart Hall, in a profoundly different context – 'an effort to think against what I find in myself'.

I started writing them while working as a Development Officer at the National Lottery Heritage Fund. During that time, I criss-crossed the home counties by train visiting historic dockyards, collections of taxidermy, imperilled churches and landscaped estates. Only slowly did I come alive to the stories of power told by these remnants. Only slowly – embarrassingly slowly – did I realise how much my own appreciation, learnt in childhood as a white, middle-class boy, worked to keep that power concealed. My nostalgia was ideological, a form of what Michel Rolph-Trouillot calls 'false innocence'.

During the centenary commemorations of the First World War, my emerging disturbance came to a centre in the symbol of the poppy – 'who bridges forgetfulness and memory', as Zaffar Kunial phrases it. The horror of the First World War is continually gone over under the sign of that flower and yet the wars in which Britain forced opium on China, occupied Hong Kong, and destroyed – under Lord Elgin's orders – the Summer Palace in Beijing are almost wholly erased from British consciousness. The totems of remembering are always, also, sites of suppression.

I want my poems to bring to light the mesh of desire, forgetfulness and naivety heritage inculcates in subjects – inculcates in me. I also want them to shake off the deadening enticements of memorial sentimentality and its hypocrisy – complacent solemnity on Remembrance Sunday, the consolations of a scone at Chartwell. How does heritage operate in the construction of imperial nostalgia, colluding in its figuration as something innocent? How does imperial nostalgia operate in the construction of personal longing? How is personal longing blended with heritage in ways which conceal power and reproduce whiteness?

This opens onto a wider field. The exploration of memory and forgetting in the context of lived experience, the apocryphal tales of family history and the transhistorical emblems of the social imaginary. I am fascinated by the relationship between memory and repetition: how repetition as quotation (indicated in this selection by italics), as form, and as patterning in language within and across poems mirrors the way in which memories themselves are repetitions; how repetitions are sometimes memories unrecognised as such. The figure of the ghost or the vampire.

And the idea of the past as a place we haunt from the present, in movement and in language, is also central for me. The work of Jay Bernard and Eavan Boland is a huge inspiration in this regard. I am interested in places, archival materials and proper nouns as forms and sites of haunting, both in themselves, and in the spatial and temporal hallucinations that can be brought on by moving between them.

When Black Lives Matter protesters tore down the slaver Edward Colston's statue in Bristol on 7 June 2020, the reactionary outcry in response made clear how much more establishment heritage has to do with forgetting than remembering. 'Memory is no good / to triumphant civilizations', writes Vahni Capildeo in 'Odyssey Calling'. In these poems, I am trying to stir memory awake.

from *FAMILY TREE*

In Vlad Dracul's
veins – from whom
great uncle George
claimed our descent –
my blood beat
heavily. Outside,
a new forest
of Ottomans.
I woke. That
weight. Overnight,
on my breastbone,
some force had
made camp. Now,
they were impaled
in the past. I
harboured but
the dullest under-
song – like a weak
pulse – of bloodlust.

*

In New York,
I was the eyeballs
of my great uncle
George, selecting
books to spread
free market seed
in the USSR.
*The best the West
could offer.* How to fit
freedom in a suitcase?
Smuggle, compel it?

That was his problem
but bombs falling
on the Bucharest
he had owned,
in which my grand-
mother had hid,
were what reflected
in the shine of his eyes.
Je sème à tout vent.

NOSFERATU

Odours are how
interiors make themselves
known to the world.
My father lost his sense of smell
when, or was it because,
he stepped onto the sea
at Horumersiel-Schellig,
beliebter Ferienort,
which is near Wangerland,
and it was so frozen
nothing could be smelt.
The sea and the sky,
which went on for ever,
hummed like a freezer,
and underneath was a body
of water, alive and populated,
over which the creaking of his steps
extended like shadows of fingers
across the lawn in the park
on a summer's day.

Long fingers,
much longer than
normal human fingers.

He still carries the Nordsee,
the iceland that it was,
in his nose:
everything remains in place,
as though it is
a plastic version
and has no interior.
He knows a world passes him by,
invisible supplicant,
holding cups of the liquor of itself
(fermented seaweed,
mown grass,
rosewater,
crude oil)
up to the oblivious hood of his nose.
And he loves the shapes of things,
what the mamaliga,
the dyed egg,
the plum brandy implies.

HISTORIOGRAPHY

Jason taught me everything I know about history. Once,
we were at an Albrecht Dürer exhibition: one drawing was
haunted by the lines of another. Jason explained how, not
having rubbers, draughtsmen such as Dürer would take a
sponge and wipe away, imperfectly, the form they wanted to
replace; how a trace remained.

Jason moved on to another part of the exhibition and I walked round to the other side of the case to discover that this wasn't true. There was simply another drawing on the reverse side of the paper. I can't remember what either of the drawings were.

from SERRE ROAD CEMETERY NO. 2

I lost myself and found a field
    of poppies lanced for gum,
for milky, languid tears: the yield
    of soft *somniferum,*

and standing in the field were two
    whom poppies comforted.
It was Maria Logan who
    began to speak. She said:

Be mine the balm, whose sov'reign pow'r
    Can still the throb of Pain;
The produce of the scentless flow'r,
    That strews Hindostan's plain.

Then Sara Coleridge spoke up,
    compelled to talk in turn
about the nullifying cup
    that terminates concern.

When poor Mama long restless lies,
    She drinks the poppy's juice;
That liquor soon can close her eyes,
    And slumber soon produce:

O then my sweet, my happy boy
  Will thank the Poppy-flower
Which brings the sleep to dear Mama
  At midnight's darksome hour.

The poppies stretched out, row on row,
  as far as I could see
and both the women turned to go
  without noticing me.

GURNEY DRIVE, PENANG

There was an outdoor gym
near the pier. We went there.
Did we have an argument?
I can't remember why
we went. Were we speaking?
I can't hear anything. All there is
is the gym gear and us
standing there, present but
absent. Two reeds from
the opium-dependent fens.
A hallucination from
Grasmere. I saw sailors
moving around as though
it were a film set. It was
a film set. I put on my frock coat
and turned to go. The ship
was sailing shortly.
                    UNESCO
hovered in the present like a sunset,
over the future like a UFO.

from R E - E N A C T M E N T

As I remember, I was a woman
and you were a man. I'd come to say
farewell. I was to leave without delay.
What future did we have? You were the man;
the smokers, Chinese; the drug, Indian.
My home was very, very far away.
I hoped, perhaps, we'd meet again one day.
You looked at me like a historian.

The escalator led out of the past
and into the future. I watched you shrink
as I went down towards security.
Were you crying? Anyway, the jet blast
knocked me back into my seat from the brink
of fancy. Back towards futurity.

*

As I remember, I was Boudica
and you were the Roman Empire. The flame
of my outrage burnt fiercely. Yours, the blame.
I shut my eyes in Little India
to see mist in blue-green East Anglia
rise, the fervour of rebellion claim
London, the legion slaughter us all. Shame
I had to remember I was not her

and could not die in a brilliant display
of oppositional failure. As we stood,
I knocked my cup. Cold tea made a lake.
A sea. I knew Boudica's future history.

My briefly complicated fury would
abbreviate to something pure and fake.

*

As I remember, I was King Arthur
and you were Avalon, the apple-blessed,
the island I would go to for my rest.
I don't mean you. I mean the *idea*
of you. You yourself were getting smaller
on the shore I left behind, heading west,
with my grievous head wound and a heaving chest.
The traffic passed on Lebuh Chulia;

the sun set. I slept until my nation
bid me wake: the stewardess said *we're here*,
gently shaking me. I left the cabin,
crossed the border and sat at the station
recalling my last words to Bedivere:
for in me is no trust for to trust in.

*

As I remember, you were King Henry
the Fifth and I was Prince Hal, the younger
you. I lay late in bed. You got up before
the day grew hot. I joined you, eating roti
at a roadside table. I was hungry.
You were full. We stared past each other,
the empty space between us like a mirror
and a time machine. You knew me

not. You were full. I was hollow.
The chef span dough out expertly behind

your head. A crown. For me, just bread and sack.
My roti came. I chewed but couldn't swallow
without grimacing. Facing, our outlines aligned.
But you'd grown up. And I was at your back.

*

As I remember, I wept as your head
came off, rubbing the tears into my face.
O Essex, you paragon of disgrace.
Too long deferred, our hopes had died. You dead,
they lived again, pale-faced, inverted,
forever virtual. As such, solace
of the hurting kind. I couldn't displace
your face as I undressed and went to bed.

Sir Francis Drake stepped off the Golden Hind
with a cigarette and a pomme de terre,
saying these are for you, my Virgin Queen;
the worst is still ahead, the best behind,
now faith is the ground of things which are hoped for,
and the evidence of things which are not seen.

*

As I remember, I was Lord Nelson.
Leaving was a battle I'd win but die
winning, thereby coming to underlie
my win. Dying: a myth's best foundation.
Nothing better than a corpse to build on,
not even a tip-top career. Goodbye.
I turned away, descending peremptorily
into the cask in which the concoction

that would preserve my body sloshed. Brandy,
camphor, myrrh. Before me swam departure.
Doha. London. Duty-free. I cracked a smile,
thinking of the duty I had done my country
and the time I bowled a yorker with a
cannonball at the Battle of the Nile.

*

As I remember, we were not amused.
Where was our bag? The carousel ran on.
We hadn't time. We had to get to Osborne
House. Bleary in the white light, we confused
the furthest carousel with the pier we used
at Gosport. A little, waiting boat. The setting sun.
Ryde beginning to twinkle on the horizon
as the coastline and the Solent fused

into nighttime. I blinked. I was alone
in Heathrow. Morning. There was no we
to speak of. No bag either, that was clear:
the only thing in baggage reclaim was the drone
of the carousels going round, empty.
Somewhere, the sun was setting. But not here.

*

As I remember, you and I were men.
You came striding down Lorong Love, the brass
buttons twinkling on your blue, naval dress.
We spent the night in an opium den.
Our dreams that night were a strange expansion.
We lay curled together on a tideless
shore, almost afraid of the stars, the stress
of uniform discarded. We kissed. Then,

the Thames disclosed itself in the dawn light;
neither was it the nineteenth century.
We were not lovers, though we had been lent
the memory. We were gentle, polite,
disabused. Longing has its history,
however complicit, in the present.

INHERITANCE

Odours are how
interiors make themselves
known to the world.
My father lost his sense of smell
when, or was it because –
I know none of this firsthand
but have pieced together what I can
from moments when clues
have offered themselves
discreetly. There –
the smell of fresh laundry.
In this way, I discovered how
my grandfather died,
failing to fix a simple problem
with the radio,
saying – he had not seen the figure
by the window – I'm an idiot.
The words rose quietly heavenward,
a speech scroll, and he fell towards
the surface of the earth, dead to
the passing pageant of fragrances
from his childhood in another country.

Every Easter,
my father takes eggs,
ties string around their shells
and boils them with onion skins
so that the boiled egg emerges
dyed, dressed in wild red
and pale crucifixes.
You take one,
I take the other.
I smash your egg with the nose of mine
and its crown crumples,
releasing the scent.
I had said something.
The Easter Acclamation
in a distant language.
Truly, he is risen,
is the reply. An echo through
a verandah in the hills
above Sibiu. In truth,
he was
never dead.

CONDITIONAL

The day they tore down Colston, we were standing
on Marwick Head staring at the surface of the sea.
If we'd been there several days before,
we'd have seen a pod of killer whales passing.
If we'd been there a century ago, we'd have seen
Lord Kitchener's ship,
Hampshire,
strike a mine left by a U-boat

and sink with him on board.
Now, we stood by his memorial,
a castlelike tower,
watching thousands of birds fish.
You're burning, you said, handing me the sun cream.
You remind me of my dad, I replied.
His hairless, at-risk head,
array of hats. Let's head down for a swim.
A fishing boat, reverie-small.
If we'd been there a thousand years
ago, it would have been a Viking longship. Now,
Viking ruins huddled under mounds around the bays,
ruffled by the cyber-wind of supremacist fantasy
blowing as far as Vinland – North America
before Columbus, who was soon to fall in Richmond,
Baltimore, St Paul and lose his
head in Boston. *If you can*
keep your head –.
We started down towards the shore.
Over the headland, another site
stood scoured by the wind:
Skara Brae. If we'd been there in 1772,
Joseph Banks, *Endeavour's* naturalist,
would have been digging it.
Now, starlings held it.
There were no visitors.
Hwaer cwom mearg? Hwaer cwom mago?
Hwaer cwom mappumgyfa? Hoarder.
I thought vaguely backwards, Cecil Rhodes
about two hundred yards away,
my old teacher, hungover,
leaning over a page of Anglo
Saxon, the present, active snow
of Marwick Head, the seabird colony,

insistent as a substrate. I tried
to share a morbid reverie – *If I should die* –
but found this was an accidental Rupert Brooke
quote, so started again. If I die before you –
you reached across
to wipe traces of suncream off my nose –
scatter my ashes off this cliff.
You rolled your eyes.
A fulmar swung close on patrol.
You sound like your mum, you said –
talking of her ashes dissolving
in the waters off
Port Bàn – *White Port* – Iona,
round the coast from the White Strand of the Monks
where Vikings had massacred many holy men
in the tenth century,
blood pinking the sand.
Some want to burn, when dead. Others,
like my mother's parents, choose burial,

*

if they're free to choose. *BRITONS
YOUR COUNTRY NEEDS YOU.*
I looked back at Kitchener's turret.
The Battle of Jutland.
Early summer, 1916. *If I should die
think only this of me.* Or, calling from the other side
of grief – *Have you news of my boy Jack?*
Rudyard Kipling wrote the phrase cut
into the bleached headstones of the nameless dead.
*A SOLDIER OF THE GREAT WAR
KNOWN UNTO GOD.*
And, for the war memorials,

THEIR NAME LIVETH FOR EVERMORE –
Book of Ecclesiasticus.
So many men, so many sons,
down into the broken
surface of the earth, called to death
by Kitchener. I felt the closeness of the whiteness
of my skin to stone. Some imposition
hard to name. As though I was
already dead, googling Kipling's *If*,
tabs open on the constant tearing down
of Colston, rage sending flames into the police
logic of America. Above the doors to Central Court:
If you can meet with Triumph and Disaster –
those stooges dressed in suitable attire, *entirely*
white, a code owed to the apt Victor-
ians – *And treat those two imposters just the same.*
Stop looking at your phone, you said.
Reminded suddenly of what I was
missing, I stopped.
A neighbourhood of statues
I'd always thought
silent. Now I heard the silence for the whispering
it was. *If* after *if.* Not the first
conditional. The third. Soft
fall-down of inheritance. Hateful
baseline of parental love. *Yours is the Earth*
and everything that's in it.
If you'd been harbourside in Bristol
as the slave ships docked,
totting up the yearly income,
if you'd been of that place,
of that time,
why of course, my son –
this is how it was –.

We reached the beach and swam.
Our skin shone like seals-
kin. *If you can force your* head under
the water, foam like milk,
hold in the scream.

*

JOSEPH MINDEN is a poet based in Brighton, UK. His verse
fairy tale, *Soft Hans*, was published by The Koppel Press in 2016
and *The Beef Onion: a grounde rent*, a pamphlet written with
Hugh Foley and Will Harris, came out with The Minutes Press
in early 2020. Collaborations with poet and artist Kat Addis,
both perceptible and imperceptible, are ongoing. Poems have
appeared most recently in *Poetry Review*, *Blackbox Manifold*,
The Rialto and *Stand*. He is training to be a secondary school
English teacher.

In her memoir *A Look at My Life*, the artist Eileen Agar describes collage as 'a form of inspired correction, a displacement of the banal by the fertile intervention of chance or coincidence'. Agar's sculpture *Marine Object* (1939) is the inspiration for several of the poems in my selection – 'A how though?', for instance, mimics the balancing and jostling together of the Greek amphora, starfish, ram's horn, and shells that form what Agar refers to as one of her 'poetic objects'. Her inner life, she notes, 'has been fed by the objects I have accumulated around me', and I am drawn to the spirit of play that fuels Agar's object-creations. I also feel a strong sense of affinity with Agar's working methods. While it was 'short work' making *Marine Object*, she notes that 'it took me and the amphora a long time to attempt such a conjunction!' Like Agar, I spend lots of time thinking and soaking things up before creating, writing in intensive bursts.

Other poems in this selection are also concerned with objects, holding close David Jones's statement in the preface to *In Parenthesis* (1937) that he had 'only tried to make a shape in words'. 'Barnacle Oblong' and other poems here wrestle with shape, and were written during a residency at Underfall Yard, a working boatyard in Bristol. These poems are intended as a close reading of place, and of the objects in that place, drawing theoretically from the French prose poems of Francis Ponge, some of which are translated or 'versioned' here with a 'boatyard' twist. The crate in 'Le Cageot', then, finds itself 'knuckle-flung', in an area known to Bristolians as 'The Knuckle'; other poems borrow from the subtle calligrammatic qualities of Ponge's poems.

Writing about the patent slip at Underfall Yard led me to think more about 'slipping' – slipping between sounds, as in the sound associations of 'Almost-Heartwood', and slippages of sound. I try to listen as much as possible, when composing, both to the world around me and to the inner soundscapes of the poem. 'Slipway' carries the slipway's name (and the repetitive falling of rain) into the sibilance of the poem, while another slipway poem provides a sonic blueprint for the noises the patent slip makes as it clanks into the harbour. In 'Wood cuts', the close sound chimes are intended to mimic the precision of the cutter or tiller, while in 'The Crate', I carry across some of Ponge's acoustics, transforming the 'c's of his 'chemin', 'cage', 'cachot', 'cageot', 'caisette' into my own 'Constructed', 'crushed', and 'contents'.

Several of the poems here draw from a limited palette of vocabulary, with an ear tipped towards Gertrude Stein, and in 'Creaks and Sighs', the recurrences and end-stopped lines are intended to evoke the feeling of protection and confinement that comes with being on a boat. Repetition is key to this poetics of listening, and I am interested in how iteration can establish a sense of wonder, preoccupation, play, or even grief.

*

STARFISH BALANCING AT YOUR THROAT

A horn, a shell, a starfish, a terracotta, a yes, a lip, a burnished,
a thinking, a drowning, a crying, a barnacle, a wave, a heap.

Waves once wept over these barnacles that spot you like freckles.
Lips once touched the lip of this jug and hands once handled it.

Terracotta can break as men can break.
Waves break when you pick them up.

A starfish is on the lip, the very lip, of the jug,
the very lip and heart and throat of the jug
where once water poured.

An amphora, an amphora found, an amphora found broken.
An amphora like an ampersand found in the sand and dredged up.

An amphora split in two like a heart, like the rose inside of a clam,
split in two and spliced too with the objects of two years ago.

A crustacean, a flotsam, a lip, a horn, a ram, a bellow, a drinking,
a how though? a follow, an amplifying, a Greek a French a starfish *

CHRISTMAS AT THE YARD
after Francis Ponge

Winter, in the end, can be summed up by those white boats,
quiet swans covered with a thin layer of snow.

The boatbuilders work with bowed heads, shifting round the yard
like bright pieces of sunlight, puffing clouds into the sky.

Paperwork is done with mittened hands.

Nature unveils her bareboned self, brittle and branched,
silhouetted in late afternoon light.

She blows cool air into the workshop, hardens paint in tins,
strokes the yard cat with icy fingers until it mewls.

A cormorant dives and emerges in a tree ring of ripples,
a necklace of eels in its mouth.

In the powerhouse, presents are opened with gloved hands.
Faces are shining Christmas baubles.

Nature closes her eyes and dreams snow into the yard, where it falls,
    quietly,
until even the lemon yellow hull of the boat by the pontoon is obscured.

A HOW THOUGH?

A how though a why though a balancing though
a salty pointed spiny balancing though
a thing on top of a thing though (on top of a thing)
and many things close and breathing together.

Barnacles balancing though tightly balancing
breathing and balancing and barnacled
brittle blushes all spiny and together and a beginning
beginning to merge the brittle blushing objects, all briny.

A how though, a rose though, a sea though, a brittle, an a.

VOICED BY A BARNACLE

that's all I had, a tiny moment, a tiny briny moment
to latch and suck and slickly stick

when I saw it, when I saw it heavy and stuck in the sand
one handle lifted as if to say, *take me, hand*

I knew that the ambulatory period of my life was over
and that before me was my amphora, amplifying

the motions of the sea and, sessile is as sessile does,
I made my tiny briny home, encrusting myself

cementing myself, gluing myself down
with my tiny briny antennae

forehead up, tiny forehead up.

STILL LIFE WITH FIVE STARFISH, TWO RAZOR SHELLS, A TWIG, A CLAM, AND A FROND OF SEAWEED

Five starfish, one for each arm. A symmetry.
The shell so white against the black-struck sand,
almost spotless (only a flicker of sediment near its
jewellery-box hinge: o -----).
Next to it, a sand-coloured starfish: *
Adjacent again, a bright white starfish: *
near a bright white razor shell: <-----------> (or rather, half),
itself next to a larger razor shell (the image too explicit, legs opened)
stretched white, glimmering. A dream of salt.
The pages of a book. Other starfish merge with the sand: ***

arms tangled in an intimacy of seaweed.
And that frond of seaweed: ~- - ~--- ~ ~ --- ~ ~,
laid out by the sea like a bookmark,
like the sea marking its place in the order of things.

CREAKS AND SIGHS

Creaks and sighs, the boat, the little boat.
On the water, a little mussel shell, the little boat.
Wind blows the little boat to creaking.
A woman on the boat, sighing, lifting her skirt.
Lifting, the skirt, lifting in the breeze, all blue.
A woman on the boat, dancing a light dance.
All creaks and sighs, the boat, the little boat.
Three napkins on the table, all blown away.
Three seagulls surfing the breeze above the boat.
The boat is blue and rocking like a cradle.
The sea, sighing, full of crabs, rocks the boat.
Creaks and sighs, the boat, the little boat.
A woman on the boat, dancing faster than gulls.
Lovers holding hands on a pier somewhere.
Dancing, always dancing, the woman, the gulls.
Sighs thrown out into the air, blue sighs, boat sighs.
All creaks and sighs, the boat, the little boat.

SLIPWAY

Your other names are less lovely to me – boat ramp, launch, boat
deployer. As the rain slips in, sluicing over silt and sawdust in
the harbour, I think of slippages, how your name could slip to
skidway, or siltway, or saltway, or softway, or tiltway. I've seen
you slide into the water, lowering yourself with an easy song,
a sweet whining, a slow clanking; I've seen your wooden posts
sink deeper like slow-swimming fins. There are other lovely
things about you: your timber cradle, how you hold the hulls
of boats so closely, how you keep your chocking stable, and
whistle at the sight of a wooden deck. They call you a Heave-
Up Slip, but the only heaving is done by the men around you,
who lower poles, wind winches, puff and glance up at the
sky. You are serene, slipping into the water with the ease of a
seal from a rock, moving your great whale body through the
harbour, stretching like a spine, singing your sweet, sweet song.

ALMOST-HEARTWOOD

The rosy almost-heartwood of larch,
which sounds like *lark*, which sounds like singing,
which sounds like the wood could open its rosy throat
and pour forth the song of boats sighing in the harbour,
swimming onto slipways, knocking against pontoons

The grainy planks of teak,
which sounds like *talk*, which sounds like the boatbuilders
as they ease about the wooded space, handling compass planes,
talking of *cleats* and *chines* and *carvels*, making tea,
clearing their throats, sculling over boat terms in their heads

SAY ELBOW, SAY HEART

Spritsail, butt block, camber, centreboard,
aligned ribs, apron, gaff rigged sloop, breasthook.

The boatbuilders balance by curved pieces of timber
(oak for the keel, pitch pine
for hull planking, larch for masts and spars).
They let language fall from their tongues,
let it shape the movement of their hands.

Chine construction, scantlings, sap wood, rowlock,
topside, capstan, bowsprit, fender, jib, footwell.

I say *elbow*, and they think of the curved piece
of frame at the turn of the bilge, I say *heart*,
and they picture the centre of a section of timber.

Pintle, peak up, planking, rabbet, rigging,
oakum, middle futtock, limber hole, lodging knee.

The language is worked into the wood as they move,
mahogany murmuring with the sound of *canvas*,
carlins, clinker, coaming, cradle, crook,
taking on the shine of *seam, scuppering*, in place of varnish,
settling down into the hull of the yacht soothed
by the words *starboard, spiling batten, shutter plank*.

Chocks away, heave-up, nearly there they call out
in their sleep, empty hands grasping rope,
lidded eyes imaging the sight of a red hull inching
onto a slipway – and as the dream fades away,
and the sun eases up over the harbour,

the words *brightwork brightwork brightwork*
lap at the corners of their rooms.

BARNACLE OBLONG

Having been told by the boatbuilders
that there is no name for the hollowed space
between the keel and the rudder,
for that oblong space that is like the body of a fish,
the space that peeks out behind the white and aqua
hull of the boat that Jasper saved, the little hillyard,
the little 9-metre hillyard named Puffin,
having been told that the space is for a propeller,
but that there is no name for the space,
I cast around and ask the boatyard strollers,
the visiting tourists, the women with pushchairs,
the men with long cameras, the children with caps,
what they might call that space, standing next to
Win's Clair de Lune, that beautiful white boat
with the peeling hull, the rusting rudder,
and that unnamed space peering out behind,
and they say, laughing at first, looking round,
rudder-hole, prop gap, propeller housing,
and Andy, passing, says *wiggle-space, spin space,*
and Julie says *prop shaft exit,* sounding technical,
and then serious men who pass say *propeller aperture,*
rudder gap, and one wonderful woman says
The Void, and walks off, silently, and I think *moon void,*
and a laughing man says *The No Idea,*
the nautical gap, and another man says it looks
just like a bow, an archer's bow, and then words build
and pour: *boat crescent, hull crescent,*

The C, The Cake Slice, rusted teardrop,
interrupted moon (I think, as someone says *moon*,
then *moon cut*), *The Reverse D, The Knotty Question,*
spare space, spin spot, Phillip, Knobber,
and one woman who used to be an English teacher
says *aerated vista*, and one man, scratching his head,
says *The Hole & Gap*, like the space is a pub,
a beloved space, and a passing French woman says
l'aileron, the word lilting out into the air,
and the German girl pauses, thinks, says *das Hörnchen,*
and the man she's with says *back wing*, and now
the boatyard is alive with words taking wing:
media luna, navigation alcove, pickle moon,
sickle moon, propeller crevice, cor blimey,
The D-Space, thrust capsule, half moon,
and I think *griddle, barnacle oblong.*

WOOD CUTS

I do wood cuts, I work
with pear and lemon wood
I cut and sculpt with a small tool
and when I print, I print in teal

I made a triptych,
started with the cranes, twisted
against the sky; finished
with the boatyard, furnished

as it is with boats and hulls,
netting, seagulls,
the moving bodies of boatbuilders;
my cutter like their tillers.

THE CRATE
After Francis Ponge, 'Le Cageot'

Slotted in between *cabin* and *dinghy*, the boatyard has *crate*,
a simple slatted box devoted to carrying those fruits which
bruise as soon as they hold their breath.

Constructed so that once it is no longer needed it can be easily
crushed, it is not used twice. In this sense, its lifespan is even
shorter than that of its soft contents.

At each corner of the yard and in Pickle café, its bleached
wood gleams modestly. Still brand new, and a little astonished
to find itself in such an awkward position, knuckle-flung,
discarded for good, this object is one of the most amiable –
although its destiny isn't worth reconstructing.

*

SUZANNAH V. EVANS has published poems in *PN Review*, *Eborakon*, *The London Magazine*, *The Scotsman*, and elsewhere, with others broadcast on BBC Radio Bristol. She has read her work at Keats House, London, where she organised Keats House: New Poets, for York Literature Festival and StAnza Poetry Festival, and at Underfall boatyard in Bristol, where she was poet in residence in 2019. She is the winner of the 2020 Ivan Juritz Prize for Creative Experiment and of a 2020 Northern Writers' Award from New Writing North. Her debut double-pamphlet *Marine Objects / Some Language* was published with Guillemot Press in April 2020; her second pamphlet, *Brightwork*, is forthcoming with the same press.

The motto of the Federation of Old Cornwall Societies reads: 'Gather ye the fragments that are left, that nothing be lost.'

In Truro Cathedral there is a flagstaff made using pieces of wood salvaged from the wreckage of the Penlee Lifeboat *Solomon Browne*, which went down with all hands in 1981 while out on a shout in treacherous seas. It flies the boat's recovered RNLI flag. My poem 'The Penlee Lifeboat Disaster' draws on *Cruel Sea*, the BBC's documentary about that fateful night, and aims to preserve this moving episode from RNLI history.

The seas off Cornwall, and its coastlines, provide livelihoods but take their share of lives. There is a precarity to life there, on the land's edge, a continual struggle to maintain balance. Having grown up by the sea in west Cornwall, and having been shaped by so many formative experiences there – including the death of my brother in a car accident – but now having lived in exile from the county for the past twelve years, my debut pamphlet *The Grief of the Sea* seeks restoration. It harbours stories from seafaring communities – voices that speak of the eternal relationship between the coast and loss.

*

FROM THE BALCONY

I remove sticks and feathers,
the compost around my bush tomatoes
a new home for a pair of collared doves:
limp leaves, a snapped stem.

They return
to try the balcony above,
wings whistling as they rise:
flares launching from a stricken boat.

DAD'S COMMUTE

He would leave his desk at five-
fifteen and clock out
on the next three-minute decimal,

walk his 'normal pace'
to New Street where the train
would be waiting.

He'd walk to the end of the platform
'because no one else
would go down that far'

and slamming the door shut behind him
he'd sit and take his shoes off –
reach up behind his shoulders

to turn the carriage lights off –
and watch the orange fireworks
of the ironworks across Birmingham.

COMMUTE

I am here
measuring out my life in morning commutes 7.23 in all
weathers and most days frayed against the window paperback
reader folding bike folder those who smell of the rain it never
ends and not in an absolute way just as waves aren't separate
from water I am attached to the headrest in front when you
move your eyes from left to right your visual cortex freezes and
you don't see the part in-between blind for 15 percent of the
day each generation a little taller what was once a graveyard a
paint can painted closed bricked up windows the empty space
between the words when black holes pop they create a new
universe it must be in tunnels that time begins each day with
a fresh set of timetables

ELASTIC BANDS

my brother died with elastic bands in his pocket 15 of them
yellow or green small hoops for banding daffodils together my
mum has kept them since in a plastic pot with a red screw lid
that we used to keep drawing pins in or other stationary when
I was young she wrapped five around her pocket diary and
uses the others rarely last week one flew off across the lounge
and I watched her crawl on the carpet eventually she found it
intact not snapped still the same small yellow circle perhaps he
would have stretched one out into a bigger circle deep inside
his pocket with his thumb and forefinger while he was bored
or talking to someone

STUNT SHOW SEASON

At this time of year posters
advertising the travelling show
appear in shop windows:

HERNE BAY;
EASTBOURNE;
I remember attending in HAYLE.

I have a photo of my brother
leaning over the crowd barriers
signing his stage-name for a fan: *Fandango!*

But leaves fall earlier than we expect
and as the posters disappear
it's hard to believe we had a summer.

BRYAN WYNTER'S *LANDSCAPE, ZENNOR*

The dark is the sea that has soaked through,
dripping into buckets already full –
night-time in the day;
the granite blackened, the fields dimmed,
the moon in each headlight.
With each stroke of the paddle,
you tried to keep time with the sea –
the blue pulling you deeper
into the undertow. In the gallery,
my small body of water
rests in front of your canoe:
your final form, unmoored.

AT DAUNT'S
i.m. Eileen Battersby

As we listened to you read,
cars passing by through the rain
sounded like waves;
a vast, black ocean outside.
It said, I'm here, I'm here, I'm here.

ZENNOR CHURCHYARD

archives the lost
Pool, Nance
craftsman, scholar
a laminated photograph, wildflowers

inside, a model schooner
remembers the lost at sea
Procter in the Pacific –
and those we'd walked across, under the grass

LLOYD'S LIST

The bell recovered from HMS Lutine
used to be rung at Lloyd's –
twice for a safe arrival,
once if the ship had gone down.

Toll after toll has breached the bell –
the crack, a widening silence.
But the loss book continues to lengthen
with a carefully inked quill.

THE PENLEE LIFEBOAT DISASTER

I

well they're mostly fishermen
they come from the same village as what I do
this is just a part-time job

I'm pretty lucky here
the sons of Mousehole
top notch

darts had just started
everyone was drinking laughing joking
a strange note in the wind

I asked him when he'll be round the corner
we call Land's End the corner
he said about just after tea

he said it was rolling a bit
a marker on the radar
slowly drifting in towards land

I I

when the maroons were heard
stopped what they were doing
rushed to the station
only eight hands were needed

all dressed
the best he had
just sort of waited
waited and waited

and waited
to catch the right moment
to knock her off the slope
she went down and was gone

some thirty foot in height
like being in a washing machine
bouncing significantly
the ocean was very confused

I I I
a mother two children
eight miles east of Wolf Rock
together for Christmas
engines have stopped

      about fifty-foot seas

with water in the fuel tank
he was drifting faster than he thought
it was getting very difficult
less than a mile from shore

      sixty maybe seventy-foot waves

how very clean and new
the green painted deck looked

      extraordinary
      screaming
      bright pink court shoes

The Union Star was on her maiden voyage
The Union Star was the latest one

With the Union Star so close to shore
The Union Star was heading straight toward

I could see the helicopter and I could see the Union Star
Water getting into the engine of the Union Star

Solomon Browne went up onto the Union Star
But after sliding off the deck of the Union Star

      she was effectively out of the water
      two boxing bags
      trying to steady themselves
      throwing lines over
      shadows of people running
      it appeared they were just jumping

      and the lifeboat crew were out
      with their arms out

I V
he always seemed to be a free spirit
like a breath of air

she went out
and she's still out

THE WAVERLEY

You and I were new, drinking on the quay in the extended
    summer
when the Waverley steamer arrived.
It came in slowly, blocking Sheppey from view.

People looked up from pints and fish.
What is this?
Passengers photographed us and we photographed them.

We cooed and we clicked and we hugged each other.
Watched it dock.
Watched those waiting to get off.

Then, with the sea ahead, it continued its way.
The passengers felt closer this time.
They waved and we waved.

It grew smaller the further out –
that simultaneous feeling of regret and relief
when friends or visitors leave.

Each shingle-stone cast a shadow over the next shingle-stone
in a succession of shadows
and shingle-stones.

We walked home. I saw us –
two figures joined at the hands
with very long legs.

EQUAL OPPORTUNITIES

The explorer's torn coat
hangs on a mannequin
accompanied by a story board.

Across the room the lion,
fixed into a roar.
Two paws pressed against the glass.

*

JENNIFER EDGECOMBE grew up in Cornwall and now lives on the Kent coast. Her poems and reviews have appeared in *Ambit, Caught by the River, Lighthouse*, *PN Review* and *Wild Court*. Her debut poetry pamphlet *The Grief of the Sea* was published by Broken Sleep Books.

Acknowledgements –
'The Waverley', *PNR*
'The Penlee Lifeboat Disaster', *Wild Court*
'elastic bands', *Ambit*

In 2009, along with two friends – Johnny Marsh, a visual artist, and Siân Thomas, a writer – I began to create work in response to a small patch of Wealden woodland. Over the next two years we spent six full days, from sunrise to sunset, walking, sharing stories, and making environmental art. Although our collaboration looked from the outside like three friends pottering around a wood together, nonetheless what happened during that time – an act of dwelling as well as of making – stuck with me through the years that followed.

In 2014 I left Sussex for the second time in my adult life. The landscape I left behind, however, experienced through friendship, art, and years of repeatedly walking a loop of lanes and footpaths, stayed with me. I began writing poems that mapped the external geography of these walks, and of my internal geography as I made them. In addition to the pace of walking, the rhythms and impulses of oral storytelling, folklore, and fairy tales can be found in my poems.

While 'Mapping the Woods' documents a place I have known intimately and physically from birth, my imagination has always been free-roaming; I leave in order to psychically return; I return in order to experience and then act upon the impulse to leave. From my great-grandmother I inherited a mythical Eastern European landscape, experienced through old photographs, letters, and family stories. These stories, which shifted over the course of my childhood much like the borders of the region her family came from, left me with an enduring sense of the tension that can exist between personally embodied and imaginatively inherited landscapes. I am interested in what happens in the space between experiencing something and remembering it; and in what compels us to make art, instead of simply getting on with our lives. In my poems I interrogate and excavate the edge-lands that border

the known and tangible world, and the messy dreamscapes
beloved of surrealists, mapping wild places I have visited, both
geographical and psychological.

*

WALKING DWELLING THINKING

This wood has a thousand exits and entrances:
stiles, gates and tripets, gaps and breaches.

This wood is hammer-pond, chestnut and chalybeate,
charcoal and slag heap, leats and races.

This wood hides the boar-sow in a thickety hemmel;
is home to the scutty, the flindermouse, the kine.

This wood is cut and coppiced and burned.
Each decade catched hurt – it takes a tumble.

This wood is two green and clay flanks pinched
by the link of iron bridge over water.

This wood keeps its secrets: the peaty-black
knuckerhole where the dragon lies sleeping.

This wood scolds with a tawny owl's brogue
shrucking and shraping, kewick hoohoo.

This wood is ashen, eldern, and oaken
a mile from the village, ring-fenced, well-trodden.

This wood summons you from out of your house
to walk through leaf-fall and bluebells and moss.

MAPPING THE WOODS

Parson's Wood, Mayfield, East Sussex
Longitude: 51.061001
Latitude: 0.308827

*[…] woods are evidently places propitious for wandering, or getting lost in,
all woods are a sort of labyrinth.*
Francis Ponge, *The Notebook of the Pine Woods*

i. Winter solstice

(21 December 2009
sunrise: 08.00 am
sunset: 03.54 pm)

Between dark and dusk
we walk to the brink of the year,
an iron-red line on cinereous clay.

Hands cramp with cold on the old road
as we sketch and note this half hour
past sunrise but not brightening
though the rooks are awake and jigging
on the frosted shoulders of a broad oak.

Pass a nip of brandy, roll another smoke.
Make a mark
          and a mark   on the damp page.

This winter's day the wood is a room
screened by snow, shuttered and barred,
                nothing doing.
Yes, we feel the Parson's coppiced acres,
feel the challeybeate and charcoal in our bones.

Three walkers, we beat the bounds,
talking of other pilgrimages:
the vixen's path
                the vole's path
                              the roebuck's.

From the knap of this hill the wood
is perspicuous. It holds a pose:
the line of golden larches, the net
of branches the beech casts to the sky.

Count the ways in:
the tracks and driftways,
sheere-ways and bostals,
gaps, twittens and stiles.
Loop round and back again.
These Wealden hills burn us up –
the effort of taking them in the snow.

Fumbling in pockets for a pencil stub
I trace the shape of a chestnut bole,
a rosette of reindeer moss.
The doctor's lanky son peers down,
says, 'Cla-cla-donia rangiferina',
and harrups to clear his throat.
Rolls another smoke.
Siân hands out gold chocolate coins,
blows her cold-pinked nose.

By the hammer pond we peer
through the burne-washed brick tunnel.
The water races, black as slate.
Three centuries back there was a foundry
here: a pond bay, trough and furnace.

We light a cardboard waterwheel.
It doubles, spins and crackles.
The old year creaks, then turns
as with a flash the flames ignite
quick as the robin flits
across the ice-fringed pool.

Night comes early.
We set a candle in the window.
There is stew in the oven,
wine and bread and salt on the table.
Johnny draws back the curtains
and St George ambles
through the unlocked door.
We cheer as he slays the Turk
with his righteous sword,
cheer again when the dead
man is magicked back to life.

Walking home through the wood
an hour past midnight
I find a chestnut leaf
       lying on the path,

                         fallen
picked up

              then palmed

between the pages of this notebook.

ii. *Spring equinox*

> (20 March 2010
> sunrise: 06.03 am
> sunset: 06.10 pm)

Sugar moon, stiff hands flexing.
Station Street to High Street
down Fletching Street to Coggin's Mill.
The air is tepid and thick,
mist draws down along
the sandstone ridge.
Traffic reporting from the A26.
Birdsong quadraphonic;
simulcasting spring.
I feel it too.
Yawn, warming
as I walk, and
my body yields.

At Johnny's house a bedroom window
is propped open. We shout in the dark,
'Wake up lapsy!' and a lean shadow
calls, 'Good morning! Be right down'.
We take a thermos of tea, fill our pockets
with Simnel cake and tie our bootlaces tight.

6.04 am. A minute past the day's dawning
but no sun. Just grey cloud and the clatter
of the burne, rain-choked and precipitate.

We circle the rough-sketched
woodland, walking in silence.

Downstream from the hammer pond
we paddle along a reach of gravel.
Above us the bank rises ten feet sheer.
We dig in the clay for nuggets
of charcoal, slag and ore,
grubbing out a lump of iron
big as my head. It is cast
with foliage, a dainty kissing ball
made of lion's mouth, celandine,
hemlock and stitchwort.

Later we sit in a row on a gate
and Johnny tells a story
he heard from Alf Clout –
'There was a white bullock
round as the moon
who broke a fence
and lost himself deep
in this tangled thicket.
He dwells here still,
and each year in March
there's one who will see him.
And they're in for a hard year,
poor soul, for a glimpse
of the white stot bodes ill.'

We nod, make note and eat our sandwiches.

Twelve hours pass in doing
                                    not much

but walking and watching the shift
in shade and tone on this sunless day.

We wash our hands and drink from the spring,
tie three-dozen ribbons to the ash tree
that sprouts nearby;
a wish for every
bright strip of cloth
binding us close
to this crooked place.

The flat light drains colour from the fields,
submerges the intricacies of the wood
and exhausts the gaze. Nightfall
revives the faded landscape
just as it begins to rain
and we see the gleaming bones
of a long-dead oak and the bronze
and mauve of budding trees.

Still walking, homeward now, heads down
against the rain, ready to see this bout through,
we cover the conifer plantation;
make our last lap along the Little Rother.

Mud licks our boots. We walk blind
night-fallen, surefooted. Until
the path dips and there is a flurry
like a leaf turning in the breeze.
Siân stops.
          Peers down.
'A toad', she calls out in warning
                    and summoning
for then there is a frog and a frog
                    and another toad
and five, six, seven more

> leaping up from beneath our feet
green and gold on grey.

We walk   single file
                heads bowed
                and counting our steps
                with care
                on this most lively road
                through the woods
                knowing

they've woken to warmth and dark
and wriggled from their muddy holes
to mate in the puddles and ponds
where they were spawned.
                     We hear them crooning now
for this damp gloaming
is their unimaginable high noon
                  and the wet
                  and the warmth
                  and the woods
have called

                  and they have come.

iii. Summer solstice

> (21 June 2010
> sunrise: 04.44 am
> sunset: 09.17 pm)

Milk thistle is the solitary maid
settling her spindle in the coppice
amongst the chestnut boles
and bee-fingered foxgloves.

The stream is silent, stretching
itself from blue sunrise to last light,
seventeen hours long. No rush then.

And the leaf canopy is a bold new green,
while fireweed and knapweed,
ragwort and buttercup scald
the fields and verges and tracts
of common ground.

We follow a fox-track flush
with orchids and milk-maids,
make tea from pods of Solomon's seal,
inhale the rare steam and lie about
in the long grass waiting
and reading aloud.

Johnny unpacks the picnic:
bread, cheese, tomatoes
red as my sun-flushed face,
Milton's *Comus*,
a dish of watercress,
another of strawberries.

Taking off his shirt and tilting his hat,
the doctor's son begins to read:

> The first Scene discovers a wild wood.
> The ATTENDANT SPIRIT descends or enters.

Afternoon dozing –

    I dream of a woman
    sitting with her lap full
    of some puzzle of yarn.

    She wears green and gold
    and is all pins and needles,
    bobbins, hooks and barbs.

    She reaches out and snips
    a slit in the day with tiny brass scissors.
    The sun slides through the tear

And wake to see the runic heron
tow its long legs across the sky.
Rooks follow, black ribbons
unspooling.

        It is time then
and we take tea-lights
to the hammer pond
while night seeps in
        like a promise half-kept

and we light the dish of black water.

Now this small place
is an amphitheatre,
the stories we tell in whispers, epic.

    Siân spins a yarn:

The way she tells it,
                  the scraggly milk thistle
moves at night
on tattered feet. I believe
she has that in her,
to tear herself from the soil,
              to creep
close,
      closer.

And at daybreak to replant her feet
in charcoal and clay,
far from home
and back again.

iv. Autumn equinox

   (23 September 2010
   sunrise: 06.47 am
   sunset: 06. 57 pm)

The rosebay willowherb
has gone to spume.
Siân, leading the way,
finds a great web
blocks our path.
The spider – a stripy-legged man –
hovers in the corner of his larder-loom.

We have been out for an hour.
The birds are rousing.
My stomach growls.

I pick blackberries.
A hazel leaf shivers
                    and drops.

This wood was full of children
when I was young.
We built dens using cut branches
the men who came to coppice
left behind. And in the charcoal
pits lit fires, cooked our tea –
cans of beans and sausages.
We came here with matches
and small dogs
homemade bows and arrows
and paper boats
and penny chews.
We skinny-dipped
in the hammer pond,
stayed out too late,
let the glow worms
light us home.

I knew all the old stories:
dragons and devils,
saints and sweeps,
tusked wild boar,
the white bull lost
and still looking
for a way through.
At night sometimes
tucked up in bed
I heard him roar.

And yet for all that
the wood let us enter
and saw us leave
to live our lives,
grow up,
move away.

Now I think on it
there were only three of us
playing in the wood.
Sister, friend, and me.
Now three again
constructing a sukkah
of willow and bracken.
Lying inside we look up,
see the tawny autumn
leaves and the blue sky.

Later I sit on an oak limb
shaggy with lichen.
The air is warm
on my bare arms.

I feel just right,
                    at home
here in my skin
and in the woods,
up to my ankles
in leaf-mould
and sphagnum moss.

Beyond
the clamour of insects
rises in waves and rolls down

the sun-struck meadow.
The shrilling fills the wood
like a hive brewing to swarm.

And yes, I hear you calling.
I take off my shoes.
Remember we said
we'd walk home barefoot?
The ground is warm
and turning.

SIBIR'/сибирь

North has deep pockets
felt boots, a flash silk scarf.

North is a pest and
stings like a gadfly.

North has a tongue of flame
and knobby, crafty fingers.

North is round
as a malachite egg.

North is a blue note leaning
on the glottalic creak of river-ice.

North is mouthing bone
sound from a Jew's harp.

North tattles like a samovar
her tall-tales steaming.

North is a hut, eaves
shaggy with lichen.

North is a sentry –
Baba Yaga's black goose.

North bangs hard
on a horse-skin drum.

North is a frost-bronzed
wood pile.

North sh-shouts
your name.

CABBAGE*

to Fatema

Slung from a trug it rumbles across
the kitchen table, this flabby magenta fist
of stalk and leaf, this bundle of pages
flopping loose from their binding
this globe cleaved with a grunt leaning hard
on the blade and I look down on this
confounded universe halved in my hand
shout   'I can believe in the cabbage!'

And yes, lean in to sniff iron and damp earth
prod the pleats packed with butterfly eggs
constellations neat as a convent girl's stitches
this leathery, creased leaf a dish of galaxies
this bloody alchemical rose, this labyrinth
quick, keen I unscrew a jar of condiments
cinnamon sticks, star anise and clove
shout louder   'I believe in the cabbage!'

* 'Cabbage' takes its title from, and refers to, a painting
by the surrealist painter Leonora Carrington.

WONE

The iron bridge stands its ground
gathering land to water across
thin air. The drop, nine foot
on either side, holds gusts of midges
and looping light from the sandstone
bank. Early evening. The western sky
is charcoal foxed with gold. The bridge
does not dwell. No more do I and
each time it is harder to return. But
the bridge – I think it knows me
even after five years gone. My heel
strikes a spark, iron on flint
and the bridge recalls the press
of my hand on the cold rail and
the point I stop, always, and turn
to look downstream, to see the way
water shivers across a shallow reach

And this moment on the iron bridge quiets
my eye, and place and time converge and
are nested like a yolk inside its shell.
The bridge straddles more than
half my life, stepping wide across
the murmuring stream. It is a charm
against fretful darkness. It is the thing
I set my mind towards when I step over
the threshold, cross the churchyard and
down the gully into Parson's Wood.
When I set my feet in the direction
of the bridge I am already there
hand resting on cold iron rail
turning to look downstream,
as I could not carry myself across
the bridge if I had not first imagined
reaching it in my mind. For I am here,

stuck in this everyday body at my desk,
and again climbing over the stile as I write
the coppiced wood, then one foot on clay
and one foot on concrete stepping forward,
already there in mind, hesitating at the
halfway point, standing as I will always do
to look downstream   and only in this way
can I cross the iron bridge.

of gravel. Yes, the bridge is a thing
of this sort, spanning water with iron
and concrete to lift me through air
and make a place to hesitate and turn
to look downstream, feel again the rub
of the stranger's child, that familiar itch
or nudge as the mind unmoors and pours
out of my mouth and eyes and ears.

*

REBECCA HURST is a writer, opera-maker and illustrator, and co-founder of the Voicings Collective, an ensemble that creates new music theatre. Their digital docu-opera, *Walk Out of Yourself*, created during the global pandemic and UK lockdown, was streamed on OperaVision.eu in August 2020. Rebecca's poetry has appeared in various international magazines including: *The Rialto*, *PN Review*, *Agenda*, *Aesthetica*, *The Clearing* and *Magma Poetry*. Written with Zoe Palmer and Dani Howard Robin Hood: an Opera in Three Courses, premiered in London in February 2019. Rebecca has a PhD in Creative Writing from the University of Manchester and was artist in residence at the John Rylands Library from autumn 2019 to spring 2020, during which time she worked on *Speaking Russian in Coulsdon: Between Countries and Between Forms*, a cross-genre work that blends life-writing and travel-writing with poetry, fiction, and archival encounters.

Acknowledgements –
Agenda: 'Walking Dwelling Thinking'
Aesthetica: 'Cabbage'
PN Review: 'Mapping'
The Clearing: 'Sibir'

Hello. Is this thing on? Turn it off. I have nothing to tell you.

None of these poems are the kind of thing I would ever choose to write. Some of them are the kind of thing I like to read. Sometimes I think that's better, sometimes I think it's worse.

I read poetry every day, but I write poems very rarely, and when I do, I usually pay no attention to what I'm doing because I'm too busy writing. Anything I could tell you about how my writing process works would, therefore, be a lie, an attempt to come up with something plausible-sounding after the fact. Anything I say about how the writing process *should* work would be twice as dishonest. It'd be like emptying my pockets, blinking in confusion, and then immediately launching into a lecture on why *these* objects – two buttons, 35p, some lint – are the essential equipment that well-prepared travellers should always carry around with them.

With that in mind, here are six of the lies I tell myself I believe about writing:

One. A good poem is about two and a half things. Editing is figuring out what they are.

Two. A truthful poem communicates a feeling as truthfully as possible. Setting out the events that inspired that feeling isn't always a good way to do this. If I write a poem set in 23rd-century Reykjavík which makes the reader feel *exactly* how I and/or my friend Z felt at 3pm last Tuesday in Leeds, it will be a more truthful poem than one describing that day in Leeds which makes the reader feel nothing at all.

Three. I don't write poems. I write them down. If the author of these poems plagiarises from my life, that remains our guilty secret.

Four. If a poem *wants* to be a circle of text in block capitals, because that's the best way to communicate its particular feeling, then who am I to get in the way? I admire writers who restrict themselves to a single form – writing all their poems in ballad metre, or all their poems in free verse – and who find freedom and flexibility within that constraint, like an artist who devotes their life to working in charcoal. I admire them, because I could never be one. I want to be allowed to play with all the different colours. If I write three poems in the same style, I get twitchy.

Five. It may be that all my poems *are* in the same style, and I'm just too close to them to notice. The same may be true of all the poems in this book.

Six. Your words are never entirely your own, nor mine mine. Believing this means I never feel lonely.

*

HEALTH

What is that? Something honeylike that makes me lean in closer,
a tag in Latin dangling from its neck below the bloom.
Every flower has a stamen – do I mean a stigma? –
at its heart to lure the needle-bearing honeybee
doing its rounds from bed to bed, fretting like a doctor,
looping its indecipherable cursive in the air.

The poster campaign tells us *we must work to fight the stigma*
over mental health but they don't mean that. Health, I mean.
Nobody is angry or ashamed of being healthy.
The rich sea air, my guidebook says, and rising temperatures
mean semi-hardy plants that elsewhere just can't hack the weather
survive the whole year round outside here, kept alive by Ventnor.

All my friends are sick. I love them and I'm scared.
Z is sick. I mean, she's ill. *An ill wind; boding ill.*
The body bodes the way a broken bone can sense the storm,
her every joint an advert for the coming inner weather.
I want to help but I just play with words. Seeking shelter
from the rain that all at once is everywhere and on me,

I turn a corner past the greenhouse, find the blue pagoda.
In it, you are reading this. Hello. Can I sit down?
This is the closest I will ever come to being honest.
Look at the pretty flowers. People died where we are sitting.
Everyone my age is sick. I've never slept beside
someone who didn't need pills to separate the day from night.

Some of them have disappeared. Some wear the stigmata
on the lower inner arm that marks the almost-martyr.
Variegated, reads the metal tag. *Perennial.*

The sky is bleeding white, squeezed dry above the blue pagoda
but the rain keeps coming. That was the other thing. It's why
they made the garden here, after they knocked the old place down.

In a room beside the mushroom house, a TV set repeats
three minutes of a video from 1969:
the BBC had sent a helicopter like a humming
bee to hover near the empty sanatorium,
not yet collapsed. A tracking shot. There's just so much of it,
window after window and a unseen voice explaining

how the lungs would fill with what was held in drops of water.
I'd like to bring them here, my friends, tell them everything
they lie in bed and think of doesn't matter for a while,
that it can wait until they've got their breath back in this shelter
we have made from words. The guidebook mentions that the doctor
who founded Ventnor's institute for sickness of the chest

died here, tuberculosis. Yes, despite the warm sea air
and honey in hot water. Is it me or is it getting
darker? Now it's late and I can hardly see the flowers.
Close your eyes and sit with me for just a little longer.
We'll talk about our friends, about the flower and its stigma
till this rain dies down. The guidebook says he tried, the doctor.

The guidebook says so many things, but we can't hear it over
the water falling everywhere and on the blue pagoda.

CLUE

Peccable timing had me caught red-handed.
You gasped and shuddered, reached for the lead piping,
the candlestick, the rope, whatever came

to hand. When it was done, this perfect game,
we found ourselves fastidiously wiping
away the fingerprints we'd somehow branded

painlessly across our backs in blood.
Your blood, Miss Scarlet. Ask Professor Plum
(making reference to the periodic)

how something elemental as this trick
of moonlight, nature's rulebook, could become
taboo, or seen as anything but good.

LULLABY

No one sleeps. Matt living with his parents
again and two days sober, almost. Jackie

taking pictures of the moon
that wakes above the thumbtacked desk

she rests her cheek on when
she inks her picture-books

of pyramids or shapes her careful lines
of coke. It's almost dawn as Zoe starts

another chapter of the niche
erotica she ghosts for seven

cents a word, awake
as us. You look awake.

I look like something you might like to sleep through.
Richard is awake because the man

he loves is on a bed on wheels
and never sleeps or wakes. It's not

what any of us wanted.
Hum it. It will do.

THE ONEIROSCOPIST

after Edith Rimmington

The diving helmet is a perfect fit.
If anyone could make it work, then it
had to be you, despite the length of this
(tell me the tactful word, Edith – proboscis?)
       this seabird's beak, projecting from the hull
       of your salt-white and pecked-clean seabird skull.
       I dreamt this figurehead became your head,
       a plaguemask for the drowning and the dead.

I like this one, you said. You like the dark
and birds in galleries and bones in galleys.
British Surrealism, a Noah's Ark
of you-like animals. I kept a tally:
       three skeletons on that wall over there
       are you. Six cats. The feathered blue giraffe

is you. Those crows. The goose with lilac hair.
I almost said, *I like your soul, your laugh,*

a flood of gush. I would have tried to tell you,
but leaning on the pictureframe, I slipped
into its silent world, where words like *soul*
sound too sincere, or else too counterfeit;
  curse words, old oaths to summon up a deluge,
  finding only one of us equipped.
  You're snug and dry inside your soundproof bowl.
  The diving helmet is a perfect fit.

THE SOMNAMBULIST

Caligari. Even if
  I'd seen the film
  – no one there had,
except for you, handsome but shy,
and The Hulk explaining Prynne
in the kitchen doorway to a cornered Harley Quinn –

your darkened sockets felt-tipped into
  diamond points,
  haunted look
and turtleneck would always add
up to nobody's first guess.
Edward Scissorhands without the scissors? Unless

I'd lied and yelled *Great costume! Yes
  I'd recognise
  you anywhere*
we never would have met. We slept
together once, or almost slept.
All night I watched your broken, unplugged TV set

paint shadows longer than the walls
   until you cracked
   the blind. Your eyes
and clanging headache had you running
straight to the bathroom cabinet.
Charivari comes from *karebaria*,

Greek for migraine, 'heavy head'.
   It's a parade
   of noise and hate,
rough music, metal banging metal,
a chorus raised to shame a real
or imaginary figure of disgrace.

When the angry townsfolk chase
   the dark-eyed man,
   he runs until
his heart gives out. The final reel
reveals it's all a dream, the face
belongs to someone else. I still don't know his name.

MONKFISH

It'd always be late. High on Red Bull and *Blue Planet*,
Attenborough levelling her mind, she'd call
up again, still up at four in the morning,
not tearful, just earnest and wired, calling
for no reason, no better reason than to share

her latest newly memorised litany of names.
Lophius, or monkfish, or fishing frog, or
sea devil. Revision. Of course she was fine.
One time, she told me that she empathised
with its teeth. *The teeth will become temporarily*

depressed, so as to offer no impediment
to an object gliding towards the gut.
God knows why I'd pick up. Pity, or pride
in my own selfless patience? She the seashell
held to my ear, I'd listen then half-listen

like the line I pictured in the air between us;
neutral, intermittent, static. Cagey about being,
but reluctantly talked into it, *the body,*
given time and a stable bed, will change
and blend with its surroundings.

Given time, I thought she'd learn to fit
in, tone down the strangeness,
or even occasionally sleep, to call
someone else, anyone – Samaritans, Nightline,
the talking clock… *standard network rate. Your call*

is a low, keening sound. Your call
is inaudible to divers. Your call
is inaudible to all the undrowned.

THE KEY

A glass harmonica is not a real harmonica
    and only half glass, full
of nothing
    to the wetted brim,
each chime
    the gift

of half a drop of water which, in this weird aria,
    is for a moment thicker
than blood.
    Lammermoor,
this stammered
    l'amour

is not the melody I used to sing.
    Lucia,
for years I was running
    the taps till everything ran clear and cold,
running a finger round the rim
    of every line, listening

for the right ring.
    The tune I played was crystalline, controlled.
It was a lifeless thing.
    The living key
is the one you sing,
    the note that's true.

Benjamin Franklin,
    nine years before inventing
the glass harmonica,
    unearthed it too.

It calls for risk, a little luck,
   a blinding light. It is

the iron and the tether
   and the thing in flight above.
The right key, reader, is
   that word you're thinking of,
and it will let you play
   with lightning.

HOME,

like pigeons do. We follow
the pull of sockets deep
in our thick, wet heads,
our sodden radar: warm,
warmer, colder, warm.

The yearn, that sub- or ultra-
sonic wumph from tail
to beak to gut that hits
whenever we face due you
or you-by-near-enough.

The clunk, that eight- or cue-ball
of solid yes dropped snug
into the centre pocket
behind our eyes: love.
Recognised, we follow

what recognises us
by the usward trail it lays:

breadcrumb, breadcrumbs, dust.
Guided, or strung along, amazed,
stumbling home. Tug, tug.

CURSE

Greg, gently mashing the keys of a Steinway.
Or Greg, brow furrowed, struggling to grasp
a toothbrush, album, cup. Now Greg in bed:
listen for the unconsolable *clop*

that comes each night before his hopeless prayers.
Unhappy Greg, remembering the touch
of things, of people. Of his mother's face.
Has he not suffered? Has he not served his time?

Then we shall help him. Slowly lift your arms
into this poem, into Greg's small room,
into his sleeping body. Take his hooves
and wear them. Look, it's not so bad.

Try to come to terms with them, the hooves.
The uncompromising fact of them, unfeeling
as woodwork. Four uncrackable lumps
of keratin; hard, staccato, blunt.

I had them for a moment. Greg had them
for three stanzas. Reader, you will keep them
until the day when, thumbless, you remaster
the knack of how to turn a page.

HYMN OF THE ARSONISTS

Between our double shifts, we meditate
on the ancient virtues: Scripto, Eudaimonia,
Zippo. The carbon-copy form of the good.
Impassioned and impassive, *passi sumus*,
we know exactly what it means to wait,
to spend the empty-handed Sundays bleeding
radiators, yearning for the Flood
or a lighter kind of fluid to consume us.
Watch us, on our knees and silent, feeding

carpenter ants beneath the flatshare's floorboards.

Rich with potential, gleaming with pneumonia,
letterboxes empty, doors on the latch,
we're sparking up on petrol station forecourts,

praying for something to catch.

WYCH BROOK
Old Scots, from 'Lost Folk Songs of Troon, Vol. O'

My smooth brook knows
no storm-blown sky,
no flood to drown,
nor drooth to dry,

no owl to hoot,
nor flock to throng.
On old Wych Brook

look not too long.

No goby swoops,
try not thy hook;
worms only rot
on old Wych Brook.

From Wych Brook's slop
grow rocks of gold.
My worldly goods,
soon took, soon sold.

Row north, my son,
by soft moonglow,
to cold Wych Brook,
by frost, by snow.

Go soon, my son,
by strong wood prow.
Don't stop, nor stoop
to mop my brow.

To go's to know
Wych Brook's own cost:
blood, my son,
my fool, my loss.

FAN

My fan is utterly devoted and the only one I have, though whether this
is proof of my success or failure is a point on which we disagree. My fan
gives me a lavish gift each time we meet, or did, at least, the only time we
    met,

under a railway arch in South-East London, where they handed me a
    scarf of such
untarnishable beauty that I knew I'd never take it off, so I have never
tried it on. My fan curates (or 'edits') a small magazine – I don't recall

the name – which published my translations of my subtle early poems into
    the style
of my more plangent and meticulously detailed later poems, in its first
and as yet only issue, underneath a sonnet by a soap actor from Wales.

My fan is disapproved of by my current lover, who distrusts all fans in
    general,
understandably, given their years of working as a junior literary agent
opening parcels sent by fans of *X*, such as the six-by-eight-foot black and
    white

painting of Letchworth as seen from the sky which came for *X* while they
    were living in
a ten-by-twelve-foot caravan and now is hanging on our bedroom wall.
    My fan
writes little poems of their own. They're just the kind of poems they *would*
    write, or so

I gather, never having read them. If my fan should read this poem, and
    they will,
they will around this line begin to feel an itch of disappointment, and a
    faint
suspicion that this poem's 'flaws' are all, in fact, *devices* calibrated to

provoke that feeling in them, and in them alone, a kind of metrical deterrent,
not unlike the shrill, inaudible alarm that wards off dogs and adolescents,
a faint suspicion which will drag its heels towards a dim awareness that,
    despite

its tenderness and charm, this *is* an act of violence – and will love it all the
    same.

from **THE RAKE**

The Rake offers an apology

Darling, let me lay it at your feet,
blinking and soft, a helpless little wolfcub
huddled inside a gingham picnic-basket
on a cold night, on your doorstep, the fog
a clean slate, no sign of the coming flurry,

the never-ending blizzard. Do not worry.
Though it may break things, let it be your dog.
Snowed in, you'll feed it steak tartare and brisket,
its licked-clean bowl the colour of false love,
of the ice outside the window, of its teeth.

*

TRISTRAM FANE SAUNDERS, twenty-seven, lives in
London and works as a journalist. He writes very few poems.
His pamphlet *Woodsong*, inspired by *The Madness of Suibhne*,
is published by Smith/Doorstop. He is the editor of *Edna St
Vincent Millay: Poems and Satires*, forthcoming from Carcanet
in September 2021.

I write poems about things that I remember or notice or feel. Like many other people, I wrote poems in my teens and then I stopped. In my twenties, I wrote some short-stories, but that also petered out. I worked first as a journalist and then I wrote novels, even though, when I had ambitions as a poet, I despised the sort of tricks a novelist has to play to make the reader believe in a character or a scene. A novel has so much padding for the sake of verisimilitude; the pay-off comes, if you are lucky, in moments of pure illumination.

Slowly, I became interested in the relationship between plausibility and pay-off and I tried to balance them in novels as much as I could.

In 2003, I finished a novel called 'The Master'. It had taken me four solid years of work, writing the first draft in longhand and then doing much revision and erasing. When it was over, it was a great relief.

Without the novel to work on, however, I was like a swimmer without water. I had no idea for a new novel.

Unexpectedly, I began to write short-stories and poems. I know how the earliest short-story came: I was in a hotel room in Bucharest. I wrote the first sentences on the notepad beside the telephone. The story came not as an idea, or a plot, but a tone, a melody, and a set of images. Writing that story was like singing in key, adding grace notes and flourishes, and allowing the song itself almost to dictate its own shape. My job was to work as though I were finding something that was already there.

I don't have an exact memory of how and when the first poem came, but it was in the same short period. The poems began with an image and a phrase, and then the words did the work, moving the poem ahead. My job was to hold the poem back, restrain it, concentrate on the image and force the words to do the same.

It was a battle, and the method I used was important.

I wrote a first draft on a word processor, tentatively and then decisively letting the form emerge. I would go back to it a few times a day, adding and cutting. It was essential that I kept no copy at all of what an earlier draft had looked like. There was always only one draft. I worked as though I were painting a picture. If something was erased, it was gone for good. Drafting was like action. Quick ruthless decisions each time.

If I needed help, I went back in my mind to the original image and tried to work out if it was true, or if it was a way of concealing something more elusive, harder to face.

This process would go on until I could make no more changes. Then the poem was done. But a few times, as in the poem 'December', I thought I was finished and left the poem for years. When I came back to it, I could see the evasions, the failures, the laziness. I re-wrote the poem.

In the first years after 'The Master', I finished quite a few poems. Then, there were one or two poems a year. They always came when I did not expect them. Recently, I have written more. Part of the excitement is the feeling that, just as the impulse to write poems left me when I was twenty, it could depart again. These could be the last lines I will ever write, or ever cut. And, anyway, maybe I am too old.

*

CURVES

Within the body is its own sweet sound
Which starts as echo and fades fast.
In the bricked-up burden of bone
Two old notes repeat, both fierce.

The city curves. The brightest will
Is open. I have been here for years.
There are lights and wires; there is
Some beauty. It is almost enough.

TWO GRECOS

There was a fierce storm in the night,
The sea lunging at us, slapping on stone.
She slept to the beat of that
In the old bed, the mattress stuffed with wool.
Nothing disturbed her except soft sounds.
With the creaking of stairs or pages turning,
The pulling back of sheets or a half sigh,
She woke in hard fright and came
Downstairs to find out what the racket was.
Thunder comforted her, made her yawn.

That night when old Casas and mad Rusinyol
And the young crew that hung around the bar
Brought the Grecos to the town,
I warned her that there might be noise.
I sold them beer sometimes and knew them all.
And they walked quietly like it was God
Was calling out to be restored, having

Been found rotting in an old shop.
Nothing could save us now. The sound of feet
Drove her to the window, mad, roaring
At the neighbours and civil guards to help.

THUNDER ALL NIGHT

I have left it out: the beauty
Of slight things gathered and cast off.
You will drive through the night
On the road from Lleida to La Seu.

Coils and wire untrapped in time.
In time. Rivers squandered mud.
There will be marches and protests
Against the fierce gleam of the proven self.

There is no boat to carry us away.
A small rock, untidy, masculine
Stretches, falls. The wheels crunch and splutter.
I am longing for too much.

FROM THE CATALAN

It was a place we came to then,
Cluttered and forgiving. There were no dead.
One canal, the water fast-flowing, whipped-up.
There was a line of trees.

I will take you into the nest of self.
Before the tree-line, hear me out.
I wish it had not come to this.
Their hands like money, uncomprehending.

Shelter in the vein of stone.
Wisdom has strange, green echoes.
There was something I lost that time
Over there beyond the crowd that gathered.

HIGH UP
i.m. Bernard Loughlin

Between the lark and the lammergeyer is the uncrowded sky.
And in the savage brightness a scops owl imagines its own
    night,
More desperate than the harmless one that
Must come. The earth is terrace and hard ground.

Crag martins flit as shadows lengthen.
They are all utterance. Soon, they will be gone.
And the sun's round mouth will shut tight
Against the dark.

In the distance, the headlights of a car approach,
Shine with a purpose that hardly
Matters against the strength of things,
And then it matters more than anyone supposed.

AUGUST

One more day to tease us.
I am ready by then. Cherries
Are out of season. Soon
Peaches and nectarines too.

Line of sun moving, until
Its light is all exposure, and
It is time to move indoors
But lazily, like dust in shade.

Then the warning note that sounded
When she came here. Her voice with all
The years, the sweet knowledge, but not
Enough to be prepared.

OBJECT ON A TABLE

Against the hardness of light, it travels
A distance. There was a time years
Ago when there was only darkness.
Memory walks towards us, half beckoning.

The house is sold; the Folly River's dry.
The strange glistening fire on the horizon
And the lovely warm earth, reddened by use,
Combined to find us wary once the twilight came.

ORCHARD

Then there was peace in Wexford, some cars
In the distance the sole night noise.
We were moving slyly towards the trees,
Soundlessly shifting among brambles and briars.

Windows fading out into the dark
Belonged to unimagined space.
Nothing grew easily here, the gnarled
Half tended back of somewhere. When

Branches gave, she must have heard and stirred.
The wet night earth smelled rank and sour.
Sound of a lock pulled back, a key being turned.
Followed by stillness now the years have gone.

CUSH GAP, 2007

All night the sea-wind makes clear
Its deep antipathy to this house
Whose foundations I will steer
Tomorrow on a different course.

MORNING

I have been telling you this for days.
Sea light and the glow of what is open.
The traffic has been held up. Now go.

If there is a principle at work
In the lovely age-old systems we apply,
I study it. There is too much to regret

And no sweetness in the heavens' air.
One, one, one. The sound fine-tuned,
The end of something, taut, exact.

BLUE SHUTTERS

There were three shutters painted blue
And they gave on to the street
From the first floor of the long
Building. In the July afternoon, when closed,
They filled the room with shadows, unsettled
The shapes and textures, made things
Seem muted, unfinished, withheld.

From that high room, a curved stairway led
To a windowless landing. The second
Room to the right, overlooking
The courtyard, was the room where she died,
If died is not too strong a word.
We stayed with her in any case, were quiet
For a while, and then went down

And told the others what had just transpired.
I called the undertaker, shook someone's
Hand, then crept up the stairs again
To find the body covered with a sheet
To protect her, I suppose, making clear
That this was where she was, had been.
It helped to keep her private and at peace.

SHADOWS

In the corner of the room as you lay dead
The old patterned jug rested in its place.
And as the day wore on, the unspeaking
Shadows came, bringing in their wake
Ambiguous claims on the softening air.

You were smiling, almost. The small battle
Between shade and light made the jug's pattern
Blurred and vague, although it must have stayed
The same; it was you who began to change.
Soon they found you and then took you here.

FACE

Drawn chalk-yellow out of dust
Keeping us free from sin.
There are shadows, sublime inventions
While I listen and say that I too

Have seen visions, skin crack,
The fist banging helplessly on a shut
Door. Locked hollow spaces
Left there after the war.

MIRÓ

He responded to the picture's need
As a parent to a child's cry
Or a bird in the air
To a worm or a fly.

FROM THE AIR

There was, I know, some hatred before heating
Came. I can see spots, shapes, mounds,
Twisted, left-over. A crash, of course,

Would slice us in two. And then
On the water I saw - no one else
Noticed it - a piece of symmetry swim away.

Nothing else much. Some faint sounds; and the land
For sale; some dark books and humming
In the margins. And the old echoing moon

That goes without saying.

THE TORTURER'S ART

The art he favours has a hint of risk.
A naked bottom, some Cubist forms, but more
Unwieldly, more Picasso than Juan Gris.

Under the sweetness of his homely gaze,
The paintings conform. Nothing white,
Nothing withheld or pale. Instead,

A mess of squiggles, a maze
Of marks and dots, a wildness in the paint,
A love of gesture, filling every space.

The lopsided look of one depicted face
Suggests the torturer does not fear pain
Or wants it just enough to make its mark.

In his house, as guests, we sip and smile.
He dealt with those he needed to defeat.
Freed, he bows and caters for our needs.

AMERICAN POEM

Hedi thinks
I am
middle of the road.
But who
will tell
him
that today
when I had
a token
for one paperback
at McNally
Jackson
I picked
'Not Me'
by Eileen Myles?
At the register
for one second
when the assistant
looked at the
book and
then at
me
I felt like
the most cutting
edge guy
in all New York
and some of

New Jersey,
not to speak of
Connecticut,
and then –
what could I do? –
I went
back to my
road and
I lay down
right on
the broken line
with my arms
outstretched.

DECEMBER

I wondered that December day
What I would miss. December light:
The air liquid and grey
An hour before the ambiguous hour.

Time when the mind's half-filled with dreams.
The gift of pure dazzling consciousness.
Some books. And music, not to be heard again.
The touch of flesh, your hand.

When I first heard talk of death
I was eight, just in from school,
And my mother, staring in the mirror, said
That my father would die, and soon he did.

From then I did not put my trust
In anything much. When I summon up the names
Of ones I love, for example, I recoil
At having to whisper what has remained unsaid.

LOVE SET YOU GOING

My heart is watching and weakening
Mercilessly counting the beats;
It is bored, casually waiting
For this to cease.

My father died at fifty-three.
Vessels leaked in his brain.
Then arteries weakened.
He moaned in pain.

My mother's eyes were grey as his
Were blue. Her breath
Rose high over the town
Before it sank in death.

I have their two weak hearts in one
Weak heart, their eyes merged in my gaze.
His slow smile, her soft side-glance
Oversee my days.

IN MEMORIAM

Her friends are coming up the hill
As she sits in her easy chair
And talks as though the evening will
Dim gently as the dimming fire.

Outside there is a wooden box
Where she will lie until time ends.
Now we hear some mourners' knocks
And they come in and night descends.

Slowly, we lift her from her place
And lead her to the crowded hall.
We put her firmly in the case,
Nail down the top once and for all.

ORPHEUS

Orpheus came to this house
On an August Bank Holiday weekend.
He made no fuss; it was as if
I had called a plumber, or a man

To fix the roof. From the roof,
He could expand his horizons -
Raven Point to the south;
Rosslare Harbour; Tuskar Rock

Holding its breath in the light.
When Orpheus pushed the open door
Flicked through the cd's,
Fumbled with the sound system,

And put on *Das Lied von der Erde* -
The Kathleen Ferrier version -
I could have told him what it
Would do to the room.

The woodwind holds back
And soars again, knowing
That her voice will break up
Whatever peace there was here.

Orpheus will go to the cliff
And call the dead to come
To us from the sea where
They have been swimming.

He will promise my mother
The music. But she is checking
The water, to see how cold it is,
Then wading out before turning

And giving me a look,
Dismissive, distant,
And then floating away,
Unenticed by the song.

IN SAN CLEMENTE

Dripping water and the smell of darkness.
This is where I will go. Follow me now.

Time pressed down, led down,
Down as the steps lead down.
I will go into the dark without you.

Below this below there is more
And it is below that I belong to.
Don't follow me further. Move away.
Don't follow me further.

*

COLM TÓIBÍN is the author of nine novels and two collections
of stories. His work has been translated into more than thirty
languages. He is a contributing editor at the *London Review
of Books*, the Irene and Sidney B. Silverman Professor of
the Humanities at Columbia University, and Chancellor of
Liverpool University.

MS. Digby 102, held in the collection of the Bodleian Library, contains a poem called 'The Descryvying of Mannes Membres'. An early (and somewhat literal) employment of the metaphor of the body politic, the poem compares the various parts of the body to the various stations or roles within late medieval English society. So, the neck or throat, through which reasoned speech emanates and around which the hangman's noose is tied becomes the corollary of the judges. The feet, whose hard labour supports the rest of the body, are likened to the farmers. As the poem progresses, the 'membres' of the body tire of their predetermined functions and a disagreement breaks out between them, bringing the health of the whole into peril. As one might expect, the author's solution to the problem is that the parts of the body must accept their lot in life and continue to work together in the service of the head, that is, the king. In these poems, I am interested in exploring what happens if we resist such easy and limiting resolutions, how do we find ways of existing within states of collapse, disintegration and indeterminacy.

I find it telling that in 'The Descryvying of Mannes Membres' the initial source of the disagreement, the first 'membre' to voice a dissenting opinion, is the 'wombe', here used to mean stomach, but perhaps not entirely detached from its gendered connotations. Eating is the act that we do most frequently which forces us to confront the porous and provisional nature of our bodies. Of course, it is not the only such act: sex does much the same thing, and this is most likely why the two are never quite distinct from each other in my work. And while we're on the subject, I'll say that I am a queer poet, not a poet who is queer. For me, queerness is never a subject matter, but a way of looking, a perspective, a formal approach, a syntax: 'Keenly, it is relational and strange', Eve

Kosofsky Sedgwick's concise non-definition of queer, is the closest thing to a maxim I will allow myself.

Medbh McGuckian, whose gnomic and sensual work was an important early introduction for me to the possibilities of poetry, took a quote from Picasso as a pointed epigraph to her 1994 collection *Captain Lavender*: 'I have not painted the war... but I have no doubt that the war is in... these paintings I have done.' Her early work had been criticised for what some critics saw as the abdication of her responsibility to write about the conflict in the North of Ireland. This criticism was, by and large, the result of a misogynistic blindness to the radical, though implicit, politics of McGuckian's feminine (though not necessarily feminist) approach to the Irish poetic tradition. I bring this up because I feel that I must acknowledge that these poems are the result of the time and place in which I came to consciousness. The North of Ireland that I come from was peaceful, but uneasily so. Although I feel no compulsion to write about the conflict in any direct way, some of these poems are attempts to read the marks left by history on the environment and on the language through which we see it.

*

REHYDRATING MUSHROOMS

I'm thinking of how mushrooms will haunt a wet log like bulbous ghosts;
of how a mushroom may be considered a travesty of a flower

in the way that a wolf may be a travesty of a grandmother. Personally, I don't
believe in ghosts, but it has been three months since a man was shot

in a street just next to where I live, & now it seems the ghosts are
      everywhere:
in clouds that stay around the fringes of the sky, in a blur in a photograph

when the camera jerked away, in a thumb-print smudge on my glasses-lens.
When I add water the mushrooms swirl like dull confetti. They begin to
      print

themselves onto the water, their flavour. A week without rain is enough
to set my skin ticking, so when it comes – prefigured by the smell of it

& thunder playing at the edges of earshot – I go out to greet it
in a tracing-paper-thin dress, no tights,

& it falls on my head like a bolt of gauze & in undisclosed locations
bodies seep into the water-table. It is the first Monday of June, 2016.

PITCHER PLANTS

I loved them, when I was too young
to think of condoms as I saw them
bunched & hanging from the iron
skeleton of the old greenhouse.
Like quicksand they occupied
more space inside my head
than they have come to warrant.
I thought *balloon*. I thought *soft bell*
with a liquid middle. I thought
wet glove for a single finger.
I knew they do what mouths do
but I didn't know the half
of what a mouth could do. & now
I can't decide if I want to live
like this lipped trumpet,
whose only closure is a leaf-thin leaf
that isn't big enough to plug
its open throat, & who accepts
whatever comes its way – the living,
the dead, & all their mixed excretions.
That there is grace in suffering
is not an excuse for suffering.
I know this. I know my jaw
when it aches, I know my teeth.

KATSU IKA ODORI-DON

I know what animates this bunch of tentacles:
it's just the salt in the soy filling the blanks in the dead nerves.

I tell myself this, but as the GIF keeps looping
through the same few frames, the same pattern of flicks & wiggles,

it's difficult to not imagine necromancy, or worse,
the dumb protest of a lump of brain-stem.

At any moment I could stop this wonky, eight-limbed Charleston,
not by eating it but by closing the tab. I tell myself this.

Is it empathy that's stopping me, a sense of duty
to bear witness & attend to the whims of the dead,

no matter how random? Not quite. Maybe it's envy
or aspiration that keeps me watching. But do I envy

the hand that pours the sauce & turns this stump of a squid
into its own erratic puppet, or aspire to be as pliable

as the clump of tissue that receives its grace?
If, as the physician says, the soul weighs twenty-one grams,

it seems important that we find a way
to figure out how much of this is sodium

& therefore how much of us is lost in a fit of crying,
or passed back & forth throughout a night of sex.

It will take perhaps a minute for the last shudders
to peter out & the tentacles to lie still again.

I want to know is it best to wait before you start
the process of dismantling the legs with your chopsticks

& testing each one for its flavour; or is the reciprocity
of your tongue's movements part of the pleasure of the dish?

When the time comes, feel free to keep a limb of mine
& drench it with soy if you feel lonely.

A SNAIL

Imagine the effort it would take to go on living inside a skin so barely-
    there, so thin
you are required to coat yourself in mucus to stop your wet interior from
    leaking out.

It's this that comes to mind when I go into the kitchen & see this chalky
    leaving on the tiles.
It is the graphy in choreo – some creature's slow & frilled propulsion
    across the floor

preserved as kinks & loops, as gradations in the thickness of the line. Oh,
I'm almost reluctant to scoop the bastard up in the bowl of a spoon &
    whip it over the fence.

Speranza believed there might be something worth reading in the patterns
    left behind by snails.
She advised to place one on a plate of flour & leave it overnight. When
    you return,

you should find there etched a letter, the initial of the man you'll marry.
I've waited long enough. I scrub it off & watch the water, a slick of light
    on the tiles, evaporate.

VERMEER'S SUPPER AT EMMAUS

There is the old white jug
& a whisper of glass in front of it.

There is bread with its mottled interior
& the slurred reflections on silverware.

There is a window cut into the whitewashed wall
whose corner rhymes with the folds

of the cloth that hangs from the table
& remembers the cupboard where it was stored.

There is a figure in yellow & another in blue,
& if you dug a biopsy from each, you'd find

the yellow is lead & tin,
the blue is ultramarine.

Which is just as you'd expect.
What's there is there

& people always want what isn't there.
& so, he painted Christ

with His forehead wide & flat below His thinning hair,
His eyes sunk deep into His skull.

He worked for seven months to get it right.
He took six years to learn to get it wrong.

VIANDE

after Hippolyte Flandarin's 'Theseus Recognised by his Father'

The chef on TV takes a knife & teases a curl of meat
from the slab of rump, rolls it & bites it, says 'in France
we like it so pink it's blue. We like it mooing',

& I'm inclined to agree when, after a minute each side
in a pan foamy with liquid butter, he cuts through the middle
& the camera pulls its focus gorgeously towards

the plate. I remember, then, I'm a vegetarian – but oh!
the browned edges, the centre the colour of porphyry,
the blood pooling like an accidental sauce.

I'm too hungry. I switch the damn thing off.
The light in the fridge falls on mounds of pointless vegetables.
Le Journal des Artistes described 'the plate of cutlets

used to hide the natural parts of Theseus' as
'a grotesque form of composition, a ridiculous idea'.
Solomon-Goddeau proposes this as the moment

when the pale, hard bodies described by Ingres
& David were 'de-cathected', when, as you might say,
the pan slipped from the heat, the butter became solid again.

Some days you can make do with mushrooms. Other days
you eat until your stomach sulks & still your tongue
wants to taste everything, to find something to remind itself.

Of what? & more importantly, just what does Theseus
think he's doing using a sword to carve the roast?
One day blood will fall as rain or maybe it won't.

PAVLOVA

It has such ease; it holds
its shape like a cat: bonelessly

relaxed. Do I resent it? Its gloss.
How it resists the whip

by loving it. To spread
is to begin negotiations;

it clings to the spoon
like history.

It goes coral-hard in the oven
& waits for morning

when I'll pick it up & tap
its base & judge it.

Sometimes I think the fact
that I am still alive

is a sign of my own
lack of conviction.

AUBADE WITH HALF A LEMON
ON THE SUMMER SOLSTICE

Sleep was a paltry wafer
after we'd come back
from watching the tide
expose the beach's softer
districts & the sun
beginning to spill through
a murder-hole in an
architrave of clouds. The
open half of a lemon had
been left in the kitchen,
weeping into the grain of
the table. The table
corresponds with the
woody pips; the lemon
corresponds with a
breakfast of fried eggs &
butter melting into a slice
of toast. It donated its
other half to the piquancy
of gin & tonics. I squeeze
out what's left of the juice
& a paper cut I didn't know
I had begins to sing
Puccini's Vissi d'Arte.

POEM ON THE FIRST WARM DAY
OF THE YEAR

The carrots might yet
find themselves in a
soup incandescent with
chilli flakes & cumin
seeds, but then again
maybe we'll leave them
to their cellophane
bivouac in the fridge
& go out late in the
morning for coffee or
milkshakes & maybe the
willows in the Botanic
Gardens with their
branches shimmying
like a good, thick wig
will invite us to sit on
the grass & we couldn't
possibly refuse, but by
then our faces will be
exactly like the carrots
as they give themselves
up to the butter & the
heat, so we'll cross
the river in search of
ice-cream, then walk
around the park until
our legs resent us, &
to reward their patient
service we'll stop on a
bench & smoke & one
of us will remind the

other about the pub
on the route home but
when – finally! – we
find a seat on the terrace
we'll decide that all we
want is a glass of Coke
& the froth will taste
like the beard of God.

ROSE GARDEN WITH MEN

Perfume is just the flowers' way of flirting.
In this they are much like us.
Like us they wait until the summer,
& then they wait until the sun
is half obscured by the western hills.
So walking home through the park
with the sprinklers chirping
like giant crickets,
I found myself in a haze
of fragrant conversation.
In the rose garden two men
were nicking off the flower heads
which had given up on being red,
or yellow, or white
& resigned themselves
to becoming clusters of brownish rags.
One of the men had tied his flannel shirt
around the waistband of his jeans
& stood in a white vest,
sucked tight to his skin
which was in turn tight against the bone.

His arms were trunks of vein & sinew;
he leaned in perfect contrapposto
to swig from a water-flask.
I thought of those sculptures cut
from German linden-wood
& hoisted up behind the alter.
& then Thérèse,
her bloody handkerchief, the garden
she could see through the window
from her bed at Lisieux, her promise to
'let fall a shower of roses',
the smell when her casket was opened
thirteen years later
which was not the expected rot
& musk but, yes, roses.
By then I was out through the south gate,
turning the key in my front door.
I imagined him doing the same
then trudging up the stairs
to throw himself on his bed,
his red skin making its own heat
& lactic acid niggling in his tissues like aphids.

MINTY

For as long as it takes a single drop of condensation to roll its
    path
down the curve of a mojito glass before it's lost in the bare
    wood of the table, everything is held

in its hall of mirrors. Our faces, yes, blown up & stretched
    grotesquely like balloons,

or inverted in a green liqueur like a cartoonist's idea of alien
    life. But also:

whatever grid of bricks & wood makes up the room we
    happen to be sitting in
is dilated & wrapped around a single focal-point; whatever
    portion of the sky that happens

to be visible through the window becomes a convex bowl.
    The weather also happens,
as it always does, & passes on, & brings those other places
    where it falls into the orbit of the glass.

It reads the room. It takes things in & what it takes it
    rearranges on its surface
(or in its core (if they are not the same)) & gives it back for
    us to read.

So, fish-eyed, myopic, cataracted with dew, a map of a city's
    erogenous zones
(a patch of grass, a tree that doubled as a lacy umbrella when
    our shirts were already

soaked transparent, a room full of steam, a jacuzzi's silky jets)
    establishes a faint legibility, just,
in this green bulb. A mojito or a mint julep? I suspect it
    doesn't matter much.

IRELAND

Fog, weirdly, in the early afternoon & now the sun that's
    rattled through the window
of the train for this past hour is dimmed to the point that I
    can look at it directly –

a porthole covered by a two-fold tissue sheet. There is a smell
    of oranges
which is just the smell of lemons inside-out. I'm somewhere
    else & then I'm somewhere else

where grass is felt, & hills are felt manipulated into curves;
    where distant trees
are pressed onto the sky by rubber stamps & nearer trees are
    formed from wire & hair;

where the flesh of cows takes on the puffed-up look of huge,
    figurative balloons
(polyester struggling against the gas it's wrapped around,
    against the helium's

innate desire to expand itself into a wider, thinner net); where
    sheep's wool has long since
disaggregated into steam; where the outsized souls of
    vegetables wander through the fields.

& here I picture long-legged carrots striding over fences,
    turnips slightly out of breath
from lugging their rippling bellies, the flowers of
    heterosexual courgettes

going by in pairs knit together by their tendrils' mutual
    involvement, lettuces
graceful in their long dresses & the steroid-bulked marrows
    that try to talk them into bed.

They are on their way to join a retinue of minor gods that
    once a year makes a tour
of Ireland's less inhabited demesnes. Here is the teenaged
    king of North Street's burnt arcade

(you can tell him by the thinness of his limbs, the wiry hair
    clinging to his upper lip);
here's the bearded, red-faced representative from the council
    of doorknobs;

& here, the itinerant rivers evicted by the 19th Century's
    insistence on canals, joined,
as always, by their crowds of disembodied fish. Altogether
    now, & altogether

as divorced from 'now' as it is possible to be & still be.
    Pompously, they form
a tumbling conga-line of anima, & spread their rough music
    round the woods & islands.

By now I'm nearing where the Mournes would be if the
    weather hadn't taken them,
& I can't recall if I imagined this. My mother is a Catholic in
    a non-doctrinal sense.

I saw a city crumpled like a city in a film where some
  disastrous event has happened
in a city; birds the size of monuments perch on the roofs of
  office blocks,

a woman with a deer's head rests on a gurney & men with
  bodies
made of metal wander through the jagged absences that once
  were streets.

But that was in an art museum, & currently I'm not. I'm
  speeding past the fabulous
brick-&-iron-work of rural stations where no-one & their
  shadows wait.

The gods go on; I guess they've nothing else to do.
The fog is general, & spreads. I almost arrive & then I have
  arrived.

*

PADRAIG REGAN was born in 1993 in Belfast. They are the author of two poetry pamphlets: *Delicious* (Lifeboat, 2016) and *Who Seemed Alive & Altogether Real* (Emma Press, 2017). In 2015, they were a recipient of an Eric Gregory Award. They hold a PhD on creative-critical and hybridised writing practices in medieval texts and the work of Anne Carson from the Seamus Heaney Centre, Queen's University Belfast.

Acknowledgements –
'A Snail, Vermeer's Supper at Emmaus', *Poetry Ireland Review*, 131 (Summer 2020)
'Minty', *Poetry Review*, 109/4 (Winter 2019)
'Rehydrating Mushrooms', *Virginia Quarterly Review*, 94/4 (Winter 2018)
'Viande' & 'Rose Garden with Men', *Who Seemed Alive & Altogether Real* (Emma Press, 2017)
'Aubade…' & 'Poem on the First…', *Delicious* (Lifeboat, 2016)
'Pitcher Plants', *Poetry London* (issue 98)
'Katsu Ika Odori-don', *Fourteen Poems* (issue 3)

NEW POETRIES I (1994)

Cliff Ashcroft, Miles Champion, Vona Groarke, Sophie Hannah, Adam Johnson, James Keery, Adam Schwartzman, Justin Quinn

NEW POETRIES II (1999)

Stephen Burt, Nicole Krauss, Emma Lew, Patrick Mackie, Oliver Marlow, Patrick McGuinness, Sinéad Morrissey, Jeremy Over, Karen Press, John Redmond, Caroline Sylge, Matthew Welton

NEW POETRIES III (2002)

Caroline Bird, Linda Chase, Swithun Cooper, Julia Crane, Ben Downing, David Morley, Togara Muzanenhamo, Ian Pindar, Sue Roe, Antony Rowland, James Sutherland Smith, Jane Yeh

NEW POETRIES IV (2007)

Christian Campbell, Andrew Frolish, Beatrice Garland, Emma Jones, Gerry McGrath, Kei Miller, Christopher Nield, Joanna Preston, Edward Ragg, Philip Rush, Saradha Soobrayen

NEW POETRIES V (2011)

Sheri Benning, Tara Bergin, Dan Burt, John Dennison, Will Eaves, Mina Gorji, Oli Hazzard, Julith Jedamus, Evan Jones, Katherine Kilalea, Henry King, Janet Kofi-Tsekpo, Jee Leong Koh, William Letford, Vincenz Serrano, Helen Tookey, Lucy Tunstall, Arto Vaun, David Ward, Rory Waterman, James Womack, Alex Wylie

NEW POETRIES VI (2015)

Nic Aubury, Vahni Capildeo, John Clegg, Joey Connolly, Brandon Courtney, Adam Crothers, Tom Docherty, Caoilinn Hughes, J. Kates, Eric Langley, Nyla Matuk, Duncan Montgomery, André Naffis-Sahely, Ben Rogers, Lesley Saunders, Claudine Toutoungi, David Troupes, Molly Vogel, Rebecca Watts, Judith Willson, Alex Wong

NEW POETRIES VII (2018)

Luke Allan, Zohar Atkins, Rowland Bagnall, Sumita Chakraborty, Mary Jean Chan, Helen Charman, Rebecca Cullen, Ned Denny, Neil Fleming, Isabel Galleymore, Katherine Horrex, Lisa Kelly, Theophilus Kwek, Andrew Latimer, Toby Litt, Rachel Mann, James Leo McAskill, Jamie Osborn, Andrew Wynn Owen, Phoebe Power, Laura Scott, Vala Thorodds